BELOVED CHILD

Beloved
CHILD

A Dakota Way of Life

DIANE WILSON

BOREALIS BOOKS

CLEAN
WATER
LAND &
LEGACY
AMENDMENT

Borealis Books is an imprint of the Minnesota Historical Society Press.
www.mhspress.org

The Minnesota Historical Society Press is a member of the Association of American University Presses.

Manufactured in the United States of America

10 9 8 7 6 5 4 3 2 1

♾ The paper used in this publication meets the minimum requirements of the American National Standard for Information Sciences—Permanence for Printed Library Materials, ANSI Z39.48-1984.

International Standard Book Number
ISBN: 978-0-87351-826-0 (cloth)
ISBN: 978-0-87351-840-6 (e-book)

Library of Congress Cataloging-in-Publication Data
Wilson, Diane, 1954–
Beloved child : a Dakota way of life/Diane Wilson.
p. cm.
Includes bibliographical references.
ISBN 978-0-87351-826-0 (cloth : alk. paper) — ISBN 978-0-87351-840-6 (e-book)
1. Dakota children—Social conditions. 2. Dakota Indians—History.
3. Dakota Indians—Social life and customs. I. Title
E99.D1W837 2011
978.004´975243—dc23
2011022408

Photo of the Eagle family © Sue Eagle.
All other photographs © Joseph J. Allen.

For

TYLER, LOGAN, KELCI, KYLE, BRAD, DAVID, *and* CODY

and all the beloved children yet to come

CONTENTS

To become a *hunka* (child-beloved) was to be elevated to a high station in the tribe, and that was an honor that did not come to everyone . . . Two whole years were spent in getting ready for the ceremony . . . but at last the great day arrived . . .

The new gown and the necklace and belt and bracelet were put on Waterlily, and some long, wide pendants of tiny shells were hung from her ears . . . Last of all, the new moccasins of solid red quillwork with matching leggings went on . . . And not only the tops but also the soles of the moccasins were covered with quillwork. This seemed extravagant and unnecessary, and Waterlily ventured to say so. "When I walk, I shall quickly break the quills and ruin the soles." Her aunt Dream Woman replied, "But you will not walk." Then she told the girl that child-beloved moccasins for the hunka were always decorated so, and that one did not walk to the ceremonial tipi; one was carried . . .

Three other children whose parents were also honoring them were borne in the same way by their particular escorts to the ceremonial tipi. There they were seated in the honor-place, and an immense curtain was held in front of them while the officials gave them the hunka painting: tiny pencil lines of red vermilion down their cheeks to signify their new status. They were now children-beloved. All their lives they would have the right to mark their faces in this manner for important occasions, and people would say of them, "There goes a hunka!," and that would be an honor. It would mean, "There goes one whose family loved him so much that they gave a great feast and many presents to the people in his name." To have something given away in one's name was the greatest compliment one could have. It was better than to receive.

When the painting was finished and the curtain removed, the spectators saw the four children sitting in a row, each one holding a beautiful ear of blue corn mounted on a stick. This was to symbolize the hospitality to which they were in effect pledging themselves by accepting hunka status. They were now of the elect.

—ELLA CARA DELORIA, *Waterlily*

BELOVED CHILD

PREFACE

"Washing one's hands of the conflict between the powerful and the powerless means to side with the powerful, not to be neutral."

—PAULO FREIRE, *Pedagogy of the Oppressed*

As you read the personal stories in this book, we ask that you open your hearts and minds to understanding the experience of Native people.

We ask that you consider how it would feel to have your child taken away to a boarding school and brought back a stranger. What if that child was you?

What if someone came to your door and handed you a book and said here's your new God. What if they wanted your car and your house, and they offered to move you to a new place where you didn't want to go— would you go?

What if when you got there, you couldn't feed your family, and some-one handed you a plow and said, here's your new job. Would you take it? What would you do if they treated you as if you knew nothing, when everything they owned had been taken from you? And then they called you a mascot instead.

If you lived in a place where the hills were covered with small graves, would you get over it?

If there is a place where they keep the stories, where they hold them up to shine a light on the future, would you want them to tell this story?

This is a book about telling that story.

In 2012, the 150th anniversary of the U.S.–Dakota War of 1862 in Min-nesota, we have yet to face our history of genocide and ethnic cleansing of Dakota people. We have inherited a state that was founded by many who regarded indigenous culture as inferior and who were willing to use any means to obtain Dakota land. This legacy has scarred both sides deeply. Before we can transform a society that has treated Native people as second-class citizens, we have to begin by embracing our shared history. This book is an effort to do exactly that.

Publishing this book with the Minnesota Historical Society is a political choice—and not an easy one. As members and supporters of the Dakota community, we believe that the Society's actions through the years have perpetuated negative stereotypes of the Dakota people, contributing to what scholars call the *colonization* of our people—the internalized racism that accepts the destructive prejudice held in the dominant culture. The ongoing presence of Fort Snelling ignores the spiritual significance of the area and its history as a concentration camp for the Dakota people. We also know that as the Society moves to do a better job of telling Dakota history, Dakota people must participate. This book is part of the way forward.

Let us come together to observe the 150th anniversary of the 1862 Dakota War by acknowledging the wrongs of the past. The Minnesota Historical Society says that its essence is "To illuminate the past to shed light on the future." If this is so, then 2012 is an opportunity for MHS to lead the way in educating Minnesotans about the history and culture of Dakota people in this state. Education is critical to establishing a just society for *all* Minnesotans; otherwise we perpetuate the cultural genocide that has been occurring for the past 150 years.

For the sake of all of our children, let us begin a new partnership based on respect, empathy, and equality.

Pidamaya ye.

DIANE WILSON   CLIFFORD CANKU
GABRIELLE TATEYUSKANSKAN   ALAMEDA ROCHA
HARLEY EAGLE   SUE EAGLE
DELORES BRUNELLE

Where to Begin

If I were standing in front of you at this moment, I would begin with an apology for speaking in front of my elders. I don't yet speak the Dakota language; I'm too young in terms of life experience and too ignorant of Native culture to have earned the right to address my community. To write this book has meant a long struggle to understand why I feel compelled to speak and what story I have to tell.

This is what I have to offer: a personal perspective on what it means to transform generations of trauma experienced by American Indian people throughout this country. In this book are personal stories of Native people I have encountered in the past ten years who have demonstrated a deep commitment to the work of personal transformation. They are engaged daily in the never-ending struggle to overcome the legacy of our history. While their work takes them in many different directions, from teaching to preaching, I have found their individual efforts inspiring.

As a mixed-blood Dakota mother and grandmother, I feel a responsibility to speak about the issues that have affected the cultural identity of my own family. My mother's family survived three generations of boarding school but at great cost to our cultural knowledge and identity. When my mother left the Holy Rosary Boarding School on the Pine Ridge Reservation, she chose to turn away from her community and the past. Like many other descendants of boarding school students, I grew up in a white school that buried the true history of events like the 1862 Dakota War and the boarding school system.

When I was a teenager, my mother told me a story of being left at Holy Rosary for two years when she was fourteen. When she came home to Rapid City, South Dakota, for a surprise visit, she found her house empty, her family gone—they had moved in search of work. In the few words she used to tell me this story, her tone calm and matter of fact, I felt something shift from her life to mine. I drew it in like a breath, felt it attach to my heart in a way that would shape the direction of my life. This one story was the culmination of experience from generations in my family, just as a single seed contains the history of what has happened on the land.

Throughout our lives, we are taught, shaped, scarred, and strengthened by the stories we are told, the stories that we live, and the invisible legacies that help shape who we become. When these stories are silenced, as has happened to many generations of Dakota people, when the history is ignored, then we are unconscious witnesses to the past. When a generation cannot reconcile their experience, it becomes a legacy for their children and their grandchildren, who inherit the raw, unfinished work of their ancestors.

As we slowly wake to the reality of genocide in this country and in the state of Minnesota, the question becomes how to live with the consequences of this history, how to pursue justice, and how to raise beloved children without the devastation of suicide, alcoholism, depression, and poverty that has haunted Native people for the past several hundred years.

For each person interviewed, I asked the same question being asked throughout Indian Country today: how to heal from the historical trauma that is a consequence of our unacknowledged history. While tribes and communities are investing deeply in programs to help preserve the language and the elders' knowledge as well as programs that deal with the devastating consequences of generations-long trauma, the struggle to recover must also occur on a personal level. Each and every one of us carries this legacy; unacknowledged, it manifests as rage, as internalized racism, as self-destruction through alcohol and drugs.

Transforming this toxic legacy is perhaps one of the greatest struggles we will encounter in our time on this earth. This work requires us to absorb what has been described as a "soul wound," taking it deep into our individual and collective spirits, draining the toxins, absorbing the teachings, and turning this energy back into the world to help our community. We do this work in order to raise beloved children who will be spared the suffering of the generations who came before them. We do this work in order to challenge the values of a culture that rationalized genocide in the past and continues to ignore the consequences in the present. We do this work because these values have the potential for destroying the earth. For the sake of our children, and their children, we do this work.

Within each of these personal stories is a belief in what Harley Eagle calls the "genius and brilliance" of Native people. While each person has taken a distinct path in his or her life, all inevitably return to areas of shared understanding, including the importance of traditional teachings and ceremonies.

This small collection is intended to suggest only some of the inspirational work that is occurring daily in the lives of people who have themselves encountered deep challenges. By considering the process through which they transformed their own lives, those of us who are facing similar challenges can take heart and learn from them. We can see a place to begin. When our collective history, combined with the genocide still occurring around the world, brings me to a place of despair, it is these stories of human resilience that offer hope.

A Dakota man, Glenn Wasicuna, gave me the place to begin this work. I knew him slightly as a friend of Gwen Westerman, a Dakota woman and English professor at Mankato State University, who organized the Native American Literature Symposium that I was attending.

At the end of a session, I saw Glenn seated at the back of the room and stopped to say hello. He gestured at me to sit with him. With little preamble, he told me that he had read my memoir, *Spirit Car: Journey to a Dakota Past.* He said, "I know the answer to your question."

I was momentarily struck dumb. Which question? And what was the answer? He tapped his finger on my book to emphasize his point. "I know," he said, answering my unspoken words. "I know how to find what it is you are searching for."

He meant the years-long search for my family's cultural identity, our nearly lost connection to our Dakota and Lakota relatives who were part of the *Oceti Sakowin Oyate,* or Seven Council Fires that includes the Dakota, Lakota, and Nakota tribes. Even though my mother was enrolled on the Rosebud Reservation, she raised us to believe that our Native identity was part of the past, something she could not, or would not, talk about. As an adult, I spent years rediscovering our family history and researching the assimilation policies that forced Native people to surrender their culture in order to survive. I followed my mother's story about the Holy Rosary Mission School on the Pine Ridge Reservation back to the 1862 Dakota War in order to understand what had happened to my family and why. It was monstrous, overwhelming in its cruelty and efficiency, and devastatingly effective. By the time my generation arrived, I was born into a white suburb with nothing more than a few photographs from boarding school and a single story my mother would share to connect us to our Dakota ancestors.

And yet, here was Glenn, a Dakota man I barely knew, telling me that he had the answer. His kindness touched my heart even before I heard what he had to say.

Glenn drew a diagram of four concentric circles in my notebook. On the outside of the largest circle were the positive characteristics that Dakota people share when they come together: courage, respect, humility, and so on. But if they spend more time together—for example, if they come together to learn the language—then they may encounter the negatives just inside that largest circle: denial, fear, anger, despair, jealousy.

When I asked if the language was a door to our history, he said, no, the language is a person, a spirit. When people talk about how we've lost the language, they don't realize that what has really been lost is the Dakota way of living that invites the language to be present. This is not about the language but about moving through these circles of healing to the center that is at the heart of each race and every tribe: common man. Because language is a spirit and sacred, because you must learn to speak it from the heart rather than memorizing hundreds of verbs, beginning to learn it will open up all the negatives in the first circle. That's why so many people quit learning. That's why the language is lost, because we're not learning first about the sacredness of the language, that in learning we encounter spirit.

When you enter the first circle, Glenn continued, what you are dealing with is post-traumatic stress disorder (PTSD). People think it began with the Vietnam War, but this has been the experience of all Native people. The people we have most in common with are Holocaust survivors. The healing starts with PTSD. You'll meet people who will try to deny all of this, he said, pointing to the diagram. You'll have to be careful; sometimes people get pulled in by their egos. Avoid them; don't try to talk them into it or persuade them.

When I asked if I could speak with him again if I had questions, he paused for a long moment. He said, I have done most of this journey alone, seeking the healing needed from medicine men and elders.

"What about my writing?" I asked.

"Heal yourself first," was his reply.

Heal yourself first. In those few words, Glenn helped me see that the most important part of this healing process, and the most difficult, must begin with the individual. Learning my family history, understanding the process of assimilation, was only the beginning of a lifelong journey. All of the pain of growing up as a mixed-blood disconnected from our community, of feeling isolated by my ignorance, by my light skin, by not speaking the language or knowing the traditions, all of that would have to be embraced, along with the stories of what has happened to my family, the Dakota people, and every tribe throughout the country.

Over time, as I thought more deeply about Glenn's words, I remembered a conversation with Harley Eagle, who told me about the hunka, or child-beloved, ceremony described in Ella Deloria's book *Waterlily*. I also thought of the hundreds of children who died at the Crow Creek Reservation after the Dakota War of 1862, followed by thousands of children who were abducted and forced to attend Christian boarding schools, and thousands more who were removed to non-Native foster homes. It was this contrast that stayed with me, the image of a child-beloved and the children who suffered and died simply because they were Indian. It was in the chasm between these two images that healing would have to begin, healing for the Dakota community, for the generations carrying the weight of unacknowledged grief and loss, for the parents who could not keep their beloved children safe, for the children themselves, for my mother, my children, and me.

But again, how?

After much prayer and thought, it came to me. Glenn's generous words helped me understand that all around us are people of courage and vision who are committed to the difficult work of undoing trauma in their lives. Rather than search for answers in books—my usual method—I wanted to know how individuals had faced difficult challenges that rose out of intergenerational trauma in their families. I wanted to know what choices they made each day that led to a transformation in their lives. I wanted to know what healing looked like. While I wrestled with Glenn's admonition to focus on healing, I also knew that writing has always been my way of learning about the world. Could it also be a way to learn about healing? Not knowing where else to begin, I had to see if writing could be part of this path.

I began by seeking out several individuals and asking them to share their personal stories with me. I knew it would be difficult for people to share private, and sometimes painful, experiences; they had to believe in my integrity, trust me, and understand what I hoped to learn and share. I sought out people who could articulate their learning process, who were willing to share their personal lives with the broader community, with a sense of humility and kindness toward others. I hoped that their experiences would represent some of the breadth of issues facing Native people, with each person providing a doorway into a larger theme. They had to be committed to sharing with others their knowledge of the "genius and brilliance" of Native culture. I knew that my own learning would come not only from the content of the stories but also in following a process that embodied Native values of respect, honesty, and compassion. Glenn's gift to me had opened up a sacred space; my intention was to ask others to join it.

Years of participating in the Dakota Commemorative March—a 150-mile walk honoring the seventeen hundred Dakota who were removed from Minnesota after the 1862 Dakota War—had introduced me to gifted people who were drawn to the March as a way of understanding our history and grieving for our ancestors. Many people involved with the March have made profound contributions to the well-being of Dakota people, especially Waziyatawin Angela Wilson, one of the cofounders of the March. Waziyatawin is a fearless advocate seeking justice for Dakota people, both in public and in her writing, most recently in *What Does Justice Look Like?* Because she has already eloquently expressed her views in her own books, I have focused on drawing out other perspectives within the March participants.

Through my work at Dream of Wild Health, a Native-owned farm with a collection of rare, indigenous seeds, I met people who understand the importance of the relationship between our bodies and the earth. The lesson of the medicine wheel reminds us to live in balance; for that, we need to heal our hearts, our minds, our bodies, and our spirits. These are the four dimensions of "true learning."

Within these two groups, I found people who were willing to collaborate with me to create this book. I asked each person to share his or her story as part of the work we do in once again raising beloved children. These men and women have used their intelligence, courage, fortitude, and spiritual gifts to transform their own lives as they give back to the Native community. Without exception, they are people of integrity who have struggled, and continue to struggle, with the consequences of historical trauma within themselves and their families. I have known each of them for years, listening to them speak in public and in private, watching how they have treated others and the humility with which they have shared the gifts they were given. Without knowing, they have been my teachers. In this way, I hope to give something back to the Native community that has been part of my own healing process.

I know from my own struggles how difficult it is to change the way we see the world. But I believe that change is possible if we can learn to listen deeply, to feel empathy for our shared experience as human beings, and to treat each other as good relatives. In the next two chapters, I invite you to listen deeply to a story of the Native teens who work at the Dream of Wild Health farm and to a brief history of events and policies that have shaped the lives of Dakota families.

Kids Today

"I seen your ma," she said, a young Native woman with the long legs of a basketball player and the face of an irreverent angel. She was looking at her friend from the corner of her eye, her hands moving restlessly among the baskets of fresh vegetables spread on the table in front of her: a bushel of tender potatoes, trays of sweet green beans, a mound of endless summer squash.

"Oh yeah?" was all her friend said in reply. Her voice was flat, uninterested. While the two were inseparable, she was better suited than her tall friend for working with the people who walked past, who were unaware of their need for fresh vegetables. Then she called out, she sang to them, "Hey, hey you, yeah, you look like you need some carrots, boy, lucky for you, we got carrots." More often than not, they stopped and came over to the table.

"Okay, I'll take some carrots. Yeah, I guess I'll take some of them cucumbers, and throw in a couple of tomatoes. I never heard of kale. Organic? Have you got any regular eggs?"

Sales at this tiny farmer's market were clearly up on the days when these two young women worked together. In the lull between customers, when traffic was slow at the Wolves' Den, the Native-owned coffee shop next door, the two girls chatted. The tall one, Sierra, who drew admiring eyes with her honey-brown skin and statuesque body, at eighteen was already

The women's names have been changed to protect their privacy.

the mother of a two-year-old and lived off and on with her boyfriend. She wanted to make a better life for her baby, she said, and go back to school.

Her friend, Laura, wore her wiry hair pulled back tight from a heart-shaped face, a pair of glasses framing intelligent, observant eyes. She was book smart and street smart, and she knew what needed to be done without anyone telling her. When we needed to ask one of the teens in our program to help run the market, she was our first choice.

"Where was she," Laura asked, seemingly not interested in the answer.

"A couple of blocks from here," Sierra replied. "Her makeup was all smeared, and she wasn't walking too good."

"She's probably looking for me," Laura said. She had been removed from her mother's care and placed in a foster home, with her birth mother forbidden to contact her. While physically safe, Laura struggled with the tight restrictions placed on her by her foster mother, who tried to control how she spent her time after school and when she could see her friends. Even participating in this summer program at the Dream of Wild Health farm, where she learned to grow organic vegetables that were sold at this farmer's market in the Native community, was hard for her to do. Sometimes we would hear that she had run away, disappearing for a few weeks and eventually returning home.

The two teenagers fell silent, their young bodies outlined by the cars and buses that rumbled behind them on Franklin Avenue. A steady stream of people walked past, enjoying the warm July sun. A young man loped through the parking lot near our table, glancing sideways at the two women, nearly running into an old man who was hobbling toward the Dollar Store, his knobby fingers wrapped tightly around his cane. At the clinic on the other side of the coffee shop, an anxious mother held her son's hand as she opened the door. Like most of the people passing by, she barely glanced at the vegetables on the table. Here in the center of Minneapolis, this was Indian Country, within walking distance of the American Indian Center and a mile away from Little Earth, one of the largest housing developments serving Native people in the country.

‿〜

I was sitting behind these two young women as they talked, a few weeks into my new job as a "desk farmer" at the Dream of Wild Health farm in Hugo, Minnesota. This was my first experience working with Native youth. Until I overheard that conversation, I had seen only two attractive young women brimming with the brash confidence and attitude of teenagers, seemingly equal to any challenge. All of the teens in our summer program seemed typically teenaged, self-conscious and gawky, with long legs and feet that struggle to avoid the tender plants in the garden. When they're with adults, they talk about school, movies, powwows, making money. When they're alone, however, they tell different truths.

For four weeks in July and again in August, fifteen Native teens arrive early each day to work as Garden Warriors, relearning a relationship with the land that is as old as the fields that surround us. In this group are teens who regularly attend powwows and ceremonies with their parents, others who have never smudged with sage nor prayed with tobacco, a few who live with foster families. Most of them come from inner-city neighborhoods, some at Little Earth, others on the East Side of St. Paul. A few have garden or farm experience, while others have never tasted a fresh-picked green bean or a tomato still warm from the sun. Almost without exception, they share a teenage preference for fast food, pop, and video games. As a group, they believe that they will eventually get diabetes because most of their families have at least one person already suffering from the disease.

Each morning, we gather in a circle for prayer. The teens are asked to remove hats and sunglasses, and they are encouraged to take off their shoes and feel a connection with the earth through the bare soles of their feet.

After circle, they learn their assignments for the day. The two youth selected to work at market—a coveted assignment—help me load my car with tables, a canopy tent, and boxes of vegetables that have been harvested, washed, and packed by the kids the day before. A small team is assigned to work in the kitchen, learning about indigenous foods and healthy nutrition as they prepare lunch for the entire group. At noon, the picnic table in the front yard will be covered with steaming dishes, freshly tossed salads, a bowl of sliced fruit. The young cooks will explain to the group about the foods they helped prepare using vegetables from the garden. After the shock of the first few meals, many of them will admit to enjoying the food more than they had expected.

Here at the farm, far from the constant rush and hum of traffic, these city kids are surrounded by quiet, hearing the sweet call of the warbler and the rush of wind as it rattles leaves on tall cottonwood trees. When asked, many of the kids say they like coming because they feel safe. Several of the boys have been mugged or beaten up by gangs or robbed as they played in parks near their homes in the Cities. One young man wrote, "In the city you are faced with a lot of pressure from your peer group to join gangs and go to parties and drink. I like coming to the farm because it's a safe place and I get out of the city and out of the house. When I am at home I stay close with my family. We usually go to powwows every weekend. I sing on the drum with my uncles. I've learned the importance of taking care of the earth, and what it means to be a warrior."

But we are also caught in a web of daily challenges that are part of working with teenagers who are struggling with issues of personal and cultural identity. During the early morning while the sun is still cool, the young men are asked to hoe the rows of corn. One teen complains, mutters loud enough to hear, this is women's work. These words are overheard by our female farmer, who wisely stomps over to speak with Donna LaChapelle, the Dakota/Ojibwe woman who nurtures the kids with the strict discipline of a loving parent. She, in turn, speaks with Ernie Whiteman, the Arapaho elder and artist who guides the cultural teachings at the farm. Later that afternoon, the young men will gather in a talking circle for a discussion of what it means to be a warrior in today's world.

We face more difficult issues as well. In circle, a young man was told that his cousin was shot the night before, shortly after they were together. He was enraged, intent on revenge. Spending the day at the farm helped calm him, especially talking with Ernie and Donna. Weeks later, he disappeared from the program, rumored to be involved in a gang. The young mother who worked at the market sometimes doesn't show up because she doesn't have daycare. Another teen asks to bring leftover food from lunch home for his family. A letter comes from the court stating that one of our youth has been in trouble and needs to do community service. We send a letter vouching for his character, listing all the reasons why he needs to stay in our program: reconnecting with his culture, the discipline of outdoor work, his potential. The judge agrees. Over the next few months, the teen becomes a strong leader.

What these teens don't learn at the farm are the bald facts that have made this program necessary, the statistics that define their existence as "at-risk." Simply because they are Indian, they can expect to live six years less than the average person, die from type 2 diabetes at a rate nearly three times greater than the rest of society, from alcoholism at a rate six times greater. Because they are Indian, 35 percent will live at or below the poverty line in Minnesota. They will have the highest dropout rate in our public schools. American Indian teenagers have the highest rates for obesity in the United States. Tragically, the rate for Native teen suicides is the highest in the nation.

Beyond these statistics, however, are teenagers who stand patiently in circle offering a prayer of gratitude. They come with stories—the young man celebrating six months of sobriety who is working to catch up at school and go to college, the young woman who enrolled in the horticulture program at the University of Minnesota, inspired by what she learned at the farm. Every day we watch as they discover their gifts—the boisterous kid who can sell anything at the farmer's market, the loner who writes touching poems when asked to journal.

In Dakota, we have a saying, *Mitakuye Oyasin,* which means "all my relations." At the farm, we teach how we are all related to each other, to the plants and medicines that grow in the fields, to the deer that leave trails through the long grass, to the warm soil that nourishes our seeds. From that understanding, we begin to teach the kids about reciprocity, how we receive gifts from the plants and offer tobacco with prayers of gratitude. Many of the kids are frightened of insects, trained in the city to squash them as threats, as intruders. Here they learn about pollination, about our dependence on bees and how we risk our food system when we threaten their survival. After this lesson, one boy quietly apologized for killing a bee the day before when he was afraid of getting stung. Slowly, day by day, they are beginning to see the world with new eyes.

In a large, well-tended Three Sisters garden, the freshly turned soil is covered with a thin blush of green as tiny shoots of heirloom corn, squash, and beans begin to emerge. A Potawatomi elder and keeper of the seeds, Cora Baker, gave her lifetime collection of old, rare seeds to the farm. As she grew near the end of her life, she had begun to despair of finding someone to love and protect the seeds. She was deeply concerned about diabetes in the Native community and believed that returning to traditional foods, like the seeds she saved all her life, would help Native people recover their health. When she heard about the Dream of Wild Health farm, she sent a letter to Sally Auger, Abenaki, and John Eichhorn, Odawa, who shared her passion for preserving the seeds.

Years earlier, Sally and John had founded Peta Wakan Tipi to provide transitional housing for Native people in recovery. They created the Dream of Wild Health program to provide a place for Native people to reconnect with the land, to Mother Earth, sharing Cora's belief that our health depends on rebuilding a relationship with traditional foods and medicines. This is the magic that draws people to the farm—the generosity of Native people like John and Sally and Cora, who have loved our children enough to dedicate their lives to preserving this heritage.

Within each carefully tended heirloom seed, all of them cherished and preserved by families that once grew them as food for many generations, lies the living record of the past, of our ancestors. Recorded in their genetic language are the instructions for surviving drought, pests, and even history itself. As families hand-selected the seeds that would survive, they chose those that bore the greatest potential for the future, for their families, their grandchildren, and generations not yet born. They chose seeds for the teens now gathered in a circle at the farm.

It was the rare seeds that first brought me to Dream of Wild Health. A decade earlier, I had shown up to volunteer after hearing about the ancient tobacco seeds and the Cherokee corn. At the time, they were planting on a half acre of leased land in Farmington, Minnesota. Each week, I helped tend the plants, often working in the women's medicine garden, where I learned to pray before entering. I found comfort in this work, a sense of connection to the unseen presence of our ancestors in each seed, to the living being in each plant. At that time, I was searching for my family history, for my identity as a Dakota woman, for a sense of the sacred that was missing in my life.

Working at the farm has taught me that knowing your family history is only the beginning of restoring what has been lost: our family stories, the traditions we once practiced, a relationship with the land and the plants that become our food. With this work comes a responsibility to protect the seeds as a precious, fragile gift and to rebuild a relationship with the land that expresses values of respect, reciprocity, and gratitude. As an avid gardener who once stuffed six homeless trees in my Toyota, their tops protruding from every window, I feel a commitment to protecting these seeds in the same way I feel concern for the well-being of the teens who work at the farm. Historical trauma does not just affect Native people; the value system that attempted to destroy Native culture is still wreaking havoc on the land, the water, the air, and the health of all living beings.

Before Dream of Wild Health purchased the farm, this small plot of earth had been overworked in years past when crop after crop of corn and soybeans were planted in alternate years. We are surrounded by small farms using conventional agriculture methods to grow their crops. Bluebirds hover above the wood houses that hang along our fence. This thin line is all that separates Cora's seeds from one of the farm's greatest threats: our neighbor's commercial corn.

In the 1800s, millions of acres of virgin prairie in Minnesota were plowed under by settlers eager to establish farms on Native land. The immense diversity of plants found in a single acre of prairie that once attracted an abundance of pollinators were replaced by row upon row of a single plant. The shift to growing single crops meant that many more people could be fed a diet that relied heavily on wheat and corn, regardless of the long-term consequences to human health as well as to the soil. Huge tracts of land are now managed by corporations that rely on genetically modified seeds. The great risk to the farm is from cross-pollination, which destroys the ancient genetic map within our old seeds and replaces it with patent-protected material engineered for specific traits, often altering the crops' nutritional value.

In the 1990s, the U.S. Department of Agriculture worked with multinational seed companies to develop "terminator technology," or genetically modified plants whose second generation of seeds is sterile. Of benefit primarily to Western farmers using hybrid seeds, this technology, sometimes referred to as "suicide seeds," would have a devastating impact on small farmers, especially those in developing countries, because they can't afford to buy new seed each year. In 2006, the United Nations Convention on Biological Diversity recommended a moratorium on the sale and use of terminator seeds. Monsanto, the world's largest seed supplier, agreed not to commercialize the technology. Instead, customers must sign an agreement that states the grower "will not save or sell the seeds from their harvest for further planting, breeding or cultivation." Monsanto is the Goliath that controls much of the seed wealth—and the future of our food—throughout the world.

Not surprisingly, given the history of this country, few policymakers see the connection between overexploitation of the land and the culture's value system. In fact, most of us take for granted that our food needs will be met; seldom do we wonder how and at what cost to the earth and ultimately to our own well-being. Our complacency may soon come at great cost to our own health and that of the land if we neglect our indigenous teachings. As Chief Luther Standing Bear, Oglala Lakota, said:

> But, because for the Lakota there was no wilderness, because nature was not dangerous but hospitable, not forbidding but friendly, Lakota philosophy was healthy—free from fear and dogmatism. And here I find the great

distinction between the faith of the Indian and the White man. Indian faith sought the harmony of man with his surroundings; the other sought dominance of surroundings . . . But the old Lakota was wise. He knew that man's heart, away from nature, becomes hard; he knew that lack of respect for growing, living things soon led to lack of respect for humans, too. So he kept his children close to nature's softening influence.

Ethnographer Eugene Anderson described the relationship between indigenous people and the plant, animal, and natural resources of the land where they lived as "an ecology of the heart." He reminds us, "Without an intense, warm, caring, emotional regard for the natural world, we will be literally incapable of preserving it."

When I hold in my hand seeds that were planted a hundred or two hundred years earlier, I feel a connection that is timeless, that is not just the past or the future. Each seed contains within its thin shell the entire circle of time itself, an endless cycle of creation. As the call of blood memory reaches across generations, our bodies respond with an intuitive knowledge that is embedded in each cell. Our ancestors protected these seeds at all cost, knowing that they, like our children, are the future.

The words *beloved child* bring to mind the image of the two young women at the market and the teens at the farm who are struggling to create lives for themselves that are hopeful, productive, and healthy. Yet because they are still children, because they come from families and a community that has been traumatized, they may not know what it means to be beloved. They may not know that for indigenous people, children are revered as *wakanyeja,* a sacred gift that must be protected and nurtured at all times. In the old days, violence against women, children, and elders was unheard of in the Dakota community, a violation of the fundamental values that surrounded them with protection and respect. Raising beloved children was the highest priority for the tribe.

It's all too likely that these bright young teenagers have heard little about boarding schools, land theft, mass child abductions, the reasons why so few Native people can speak their language. It's possible they were never taught their own family history, because all too often these stories have been swallowed up into silence as generations of children bore pain that was too great to speak of. These young people do not yet know that they are on the front line of a war against history, against the invisible legacy that has been passed from one generation to the next. Nor do they know that beneath the epidemic levels of alcoholism, violence, poverty, and disease lies what scholar Andrea Smith describes as a "soul wound" that they will inherit.

Throughout Indian Country, there are signs of hope and healing as well. More Native people are learning their languages, returning to ceremonies, and insisting that indigenous culture is not second rate, not inferior, as so many generations have been taught to believe. As we return to our traditions, we begin to rediscover the "genius and brilliance" of indigenous people, the long history of science, philosophy, art, agriculture, and spirituality created by sophisticated tribal societies.

Much difficult work lies ahead—telling the hard stories of abuse and loss, acknowledging that soul wound. Yet grieving alone will not be enough to carry us the distance we need to travel; we must work for justice, and we must remember to walk with beauty.

As a mother and grandmother, I have this to say to the teens at the farm: Your ancestors loved you, regarded you as their beloved children, and for you they were willing to suffer so that you might survive. As you find yourself reminded every day of the sufferings that Native people have endured, remember that you are a proud member of a culture whose teachings hold the wisdom that is needed to heal our families, our community, and the earth. You must learn, you must arm yourself for battle, for your generation must do whatever is needed to ensure that the next seven generations will survive.

In Harm's Way

In the southwest corner of Minnesota, Fort Ridgely State Park overlooks the Minnesota River Valley, providing a tourist destination complete with camping, golf, and a glimpse of the role that Fort Ridgely played in the area's history. Archaeologists have helped uncover and preserve the stone remnants of the field kitchen that was used to feed Colonel Henry Sibley's soldiers during the 1862 Dakota War. Visitors can see the ravines from which Dakota warriors attacked and consider the logistics of defending such a poorly situated fort. The surrounding fields are rich with cannonball shrapnel and old nails from the wooden stable used to house the soldiers' horses, reminders of the critical battles that were fought with Dakota warriors. Preserving a site like Fort Ridgely, much like preserving Fort Snelling in St. Paul, speaks clearly to the way in which history is told by whoever wins the war.

In the soil below the remnants of the field kitchen is a layer of pottery and fine-tipped arrowheads once used to hunt bison by Native people who lived in this area one thousand years earlier. Revered as sacred animals, bison were critical to the survival of Native people living on the Plains, their central role in the culture portrayed through Creation stories. Lakota medicine man John Fire Lame Deer explained:

> The buffalo gave us everything we needed. Without it we were nothing. Our tipis were made of his skin. His hide was our bed, our blanket, our winter coat. It was our drum, throbbing through the night, alive, holy. Out of his skin we made our water bags. His flesh strengthened us, became flesh of our

flesh. Not the smallest part of it was wasted. His stomach, a red-hot stone dropped into it, became our soup kettle. His horns were our spoons, the bones our knives, our women's awls and needles. Out of his sinews we made our bowstrings and thread. His ribs were fashioned into sleds for our children, his hoofs became rattles. His mighty skull, with the pipe leaning against it, was our sacred altar. The name of the greatest of all Sioux was Tatanka Iyotake—Sitting Bull. When you killed off the buffalo you also killed the Indian—the real, natural, "wild" Indian.

Buried deeper yet, well below the surface, lies a circle of ancient stones with a small opening to the east. These large stones, many close in size to volleyballs, show signs that they were heated by fire until they were glowing hot. They lack any residue of charcoal, which may have leached away over time, so the stones cannot be tested through carbon dating, but archaeologists speculate that they may be twelve thousand years old. In southern Minnesota, this was near the end of the Ice Age when the Glacial River Warren carved out the wide gorge of the Minnesota River. Oral tradition, as well as the presence of spear points in the river valley from the same time period, tells us that Native people have been present in Minnesota for thousands of years.

In the time before Columbus, indigenous tribes of the Americas developed three-fifths of the world's crops that are now in production, including the humble potato, which is credited with stabilizing much of Europe's tendency toward episodic famines. Andean farmers produced three thousand varieties of potatoes while a mere 250 are now grown in North America. Nearly 90 percent of the vegetables that were grown in the United States before contact with Europeans are now extinct.

Over centuries of close relationship with the Plant Nation, Native people accumulated a vast knowledge of plant properties that became the basis for modern pharmacology. Far preceding modern-day ecology, indigenous peoples held detailed traditional knowledge about how to live in balance with the natural laws of a particular place. Well-known Tewa educator Greg Cajete called this *sacred science:* knowing, remembering, practicing, and implementing place-based natural laws, which consist of eminently practical knowledge for survival.

Among the many innovative discoveries and inventions of indigenous people are early maps that combined both the terrestrial and cosmological worlds; a sophisticated system of star knowledge; intricate cache pits capable of storing dried foods and seeds for extended periods of time; ancient medicine wheels and cairns that were scattered around the country. The list goes on to include equitable social systems, government, architecture, philosophy, and an aesthetic that incorporated beauty within all aspects of daily life.

So how was it that such sophisticated and accomplished peoples could be overrun by the arrival of Europeans? As Jack Weatherford stated in his book *Indian Givers,* "While American Indians had spent millennia becoming the world's greatest farmers and pharmacists, the people of the Old World had spent a similar period amassing the world's greatest arsenal of weapons."

The invaders carried another weapon as well. A hundred years after Columbus arrived, an estimated 90 percent of Native people had died from typhus, smallpox, measles, diphtheria, influenza, and other diseases carried by those who lived close to domesticated animals. The resulting instability in Native cultures made armed conquest that much easier. In the more recent past, a mere 150 years since the 1862 Dakota War, Dakota people have faced an unrelenting series of devastating losses, most of them imposed by the U.S. government. From the coercive treaties that seized millions of acres of land to boarding schools that literally kidnapped Native children from their homes, Native people have been under assault for more than five hundred years.

Stripped of ceremonies and forbidden to practice their spirituality in 1883 by the Bureau of Indian Affairs, Native people were left with little ability to recover. As Dr. Maria Yellow Horse Brave Heart said:

> We have a lot of wisdom in our culture and we have a lot of traditional healing practices. We have traditional grief ceremonies, we have spirit keeping,

and spirit releasing ceremonies. We have ways of dealing with death and loss and grief and trauma and purification, when warriors would come back from war. But a lot of that was outlawed by the federal government policies around 1883 . . . As a result of all this, we have historical trauma.

Consequently, we have arrived at an era in which Native people are often defined by statistics that show remarkably high levels of alcoholism, disease, poverty, abuse, depression, and suicide. Over time, without the understanding that these statistics are the consequence of a brutal history, they may even come to represent Native people themselves, forging an identity as eternal victims still reliant on the Great Father for survival. Hence the origin of stereotypes that include Native-themed mascots and an unacknowledged systemic racism that we as Native people also internalize. We forget who we were, instead tracing our families back to the 1862 Dakota War as if we both ended and began at that time. There are many families who do not yet know even that much history.

If we look at the past 150 years as a horrifically traumatic time in our very long history, then the question becomes one of asking how we can heal from this historical trauma, how generations carrying unresolved grief might once again raise beloved children. We know that Dakota people have always cherished their children, regarding their safety and well-being as the highest priority of the tribe, a fact that is confirmed by writers like Ella Deloria. If we are to understand how a people who have honored their children as beloved have come to allow too many children to live in harm's way, then we must look to the past. First, to the trauma, to understand what has happened. Then we must look to the knowledge that we also carry in our blood and in our collective memories, of the people we remain despite generations of living as second-class citizens in this country.

What gives me hope is the work of Native people who have identified the symptoms of generations-long historical trauma and have created programs to transform it. In her groundbreaking work, Dr. Maria Yellow Horse Brave Heart defined historical trauma as the "cumulative emotional and psychological wounding over the lifespan and across generations, emanating from massive group trauma." In 1992, Dr. Brave Heart co-founded the Takini Network, whose name in Lakota means "survivor" or "to come back to life." The Takini Network focuses on helping Native people heal from historical trauma, as do programs such as White Bison (which promotes sobriety and wellness) and National Association for Native American Children of Alcoholics (NANACOA).

What is especially compelling in Dr. Brave Heart's work is her development of a process that offers hope for living happy, healthy lives and raising children who are once again beloved. Not surprisingly for a community educated in white institutions, the first step in confronting the trauma is to embrace our history, which means we embrace the genocide that has occurred within this country and within the state of Minnesota. This history, which begins with the idea that Columbus "discovered" America, follows the destructive path of ruthless conquest to the present day. Without a clear understanding of what has been lost, we cannot see the unacknowledged grief that we all carry. Nor can we see that the level of dysfunction in Native communities is the result of human rights violations that remain unacknowledged by churches, states, and the federal government.

Secondly, we need to understand how this trauma manifests in a number of different responses, from depression to anger to substance abuse. The trauma gets passed on because the parents were traumatized, and we tend to parent the same way we were raised unless we learn something new along the way. Once we understand the trauma, we can find ways to release the grief by returning to ceremonies that were outlawed or by participating in events that commemorate some of the horrific moments in our history, such as the Dakota Commemorative March.

We can also continue to rebuild the physical health of our communities. Generations of living on commodity foods has ruined the health of many Native people with high-fat, high-starch foods, including fry bread. New research indicates that the body's response to chronic stress or trauma may have a direct connection to type 2 diabetes, a disease that is epidemic among Native people. If we don't address the health issues in our communities, then diabetes will become an effective, silent termination policy.

And finally, through this process, we find ways to transcend the trauma so that we no longer identify as victims or even survivors. We become free to be joyful in our own lives. To this I would add, we become free to work toward justice for our communities, however we define that work, and to extend a hand to those still suffering.

The student pointed to a single sentence in her book, asking about the anger behind my flat statement "I wanted to rip Tarble's face off." Helen Mar Tarble was a young pioneer bride of 1857 who had described my Dakota great-great-grandmother as "repulsive" because of her dark skin. The student wanted to know why there is so much anger in Native people.

I was a visiting author in her class, invited to talk about *Spirit Car*. I knew why she asked that question; I also knew the long and painful answer. In the white school I attended, we learned about Manifest Destiny, the nineteenth-century belief that Americans were "destined"—anointed by God—to dominate the entire North American continent. I read this phrase without understanding that this poetic language was used to justify a rapacious march across the country.

Decades later, when I reexamined history with a critical eye, I learned how this lyrical phrase was in fact a mask for a much uglier truth. Research into my family's history led me back to boarding schools, land allotment, blood quantum, intermarriage, missionaries, and finally to the 1862 Dakota War in Minnesota.

After once occupying most of the southern half of Minnesota, the Dakota were forced in the 1850s onto a strip of reservation land ten miles wide along the Minnesota River. Offering mostly promises in exchange, the whites demanded that the Dakota forget their traditions, their spiritual ways, and their language—and surrender their homeland. Faced with starvation while warehouses were filled with food belonging to the Dakota, with dishonest treaties, and with unrelenting pressure to relinquish their culture, Dakota people attacked white settlers as an act of resistance and a desperate attempt to remove the intruders from their homeland.

After the war, when the Dakota surrendered, sham military tribunals condemned more than three hundred men to be hanged, a number that was later reduced by President Lincoln to thirty-eight. The whites were so eager for vengeance that even the Dakota who had saved the lives of settlers were swept into the misery. While the men were imprisoned at Mankato, thirty-eight warriors were hanged on December 26, 1862. On November 7, 1862, a four-mile train of nearly seventeen hundred women, children, and elders were forced to walk 150 miles through towns where enraged settlers lined the streets, hurling rocks and sticks and even boiling water. A baby was snatched from a woman's arms, his head smashed, and then he was returned to his mother; within hours, he was dead. Those who died along the way were simply left. Nearly three hundred more died during the winter in an overcrowded, disease-filled concentration camp below Fort Snelling.

As Dakota people struggled to survive, they also faced an insidious threat from within the tribe itself—the bitterness and rancor that followed the hard choices families had to make to survive. My Dakota great-great-grandmother, Rosalie Marpiya Mase, took refuge at Fort Ridgely with her French Canadian husband and mixed-blood children. Her eldest son had enlisted with the Renville Rangers, a group of mostly mixed-blood young men who signed up to serve in the Civil War but were called back to fight against their own relatives. Some men testified against Dakota warriors during the trials, essentially condemning them to death, while others became scouts who tracked fleeing Dakota families for Sibley. The rules of kinship, intended to establish and preserve cultural harmony, were displaced by feelings of betrayal and a desire for vengeance. Even today, these bitter memories continue to divide the Dakota community.

In 2002, the original 1862 marchers were honored with the first-ever Dakota Commemorative March, organized by Waziyatawin Angela Wilson, Leo Omani, and Gabrielle Tateyuskanskan. Leaving at dawn from the Lower Sioux Community Center, a small group of Dakota descendents and supporters followed approximately the same route used in 1862. Since then, the Dakota Commemorative March has been held every other year, with each event attracting new people from across the country who return to their homeland. For many, including me and my brother, the March has been a spiritual journey, a way of opening up to the past and embracing our history. In 2006, the third March welcomed more families with young children than had been present in the past. Each evening, the marchers sat exhausted while the young children played, releasing their energy after riding in cars much of the day.

On the fourth night, a group of about forty people sat together in a large open room at the Joseph R. Brown Minnesota River Center in Henderson, Minnesota, one of the towns made infamous for its residents' violent, hate-filled treatment of the original marchers in 1862. On that night, we were served a hot dinner and provided with a place to sleep by people who acknowledged their town's history by extending their hospitality to us.

We had left Mankato that morning in the still dark hour just after dawn, a heavy layer of wet snow covering the ground. A challenge for the walkers, I thought, listening to the sounds of snow plows moving down the side streets and alleys. Before breakfast, however, one of the elders thanked the Creator for the blessing of snow. A full day's walk later, about eighteen miles, we came slowly down the hill into Henderson. At the door of the center, a poster advertised a holiday event: "And the Lion shall lie down with the lamb." Inside, a half dozen people bustled about, preparing a long table with hot food, and offered coffee to walkers who eagerly grabbed the first chair they saw.

After dinner, many of us would have been content to go straight to our sleeping bags, but it was our custom most nights to gather for conversation or sometimes a ceremony, as directed by the spiritual leaders who traveled with us. We had been walking long distances—between fifteen and twenty miles each day—for four straight days. Many feet had blisters that needed bandages and moleskin each morning. Fatigue had exposed weaknesses in knees, hips, and ankles. By the fourth day, our emotional defenses were depleted while our bodies were beginning to adjust to the physical demands of this long spiritual walk. Few complaints were heard; we carried the memory of our ancestors walking without warm clothing, adequate food, or a dry place to sleep at night.

Despite our collective weariness, we listened as each person spoke his or her thoughts and feelings about the day, moving from one person to the next in a circle around the room. Some people declined to speak with a turn of the head. Others wept almost with their first words, overcome by the emotion they had carried for four days.

Halfway around the circle, we waited as John prepared to speak. He sat for a long moment in silence with his large, square hands folded peacefully in front of him. This was his third March and the first time he had brought his young family with him, his beautiful Lakota wife, his ten-year-old daughter, and two younger children. During the previous March, John had strained his knee on the hills leading to Mankato and had often walked in great pain. His kind face and his obvious devotion to family, combined with a lively sense of humor, made him a strong presence in our group.

John leaned forward, his elbows on his knees, his head slightly bowed.

"This March has been different for me," he said, his familiar voice carrying easily through the room. "Today while I was driving, it felt good to have my family here, to see my wife and daughter out walking with the marchers." He paused while a wave of strong emotion steeled the muscles in his face. "But it's different than when it was just me walking. Now when I think about the original marchers, I see my own family. I think how it would have felt to not be there to protect my family." He stopped, unable to continue. His words echoed our shared need to protect the children.

The quiet words spoken by this young father reminded us of the painful separation that had occurred between the men and their families after the war. After the women and children were marched to Fort Snelling, the men were moved from Mankato to a prison at Davenport, Iowa. Men were unable to protect their wives and children from what lay ahead, first at Fort Snelling and later at the Crow Creek Reservation.

In spring 1863, to the cheers of hostile crowds, the surviving Dakota were crowded onto flatboats for a slow, torturous trip to Crow Creek in South Dakota in conditions that were compared by missionary John P. Williamson to those experienced by slaves during their trans-Atlantic transport. Of the 1,324 prisoners who left Fort Snelling in the spring of 1863, most of them women and children, sixteen died during the trip to Crow Creek on overcrowded steamboats. In the first six weeks, 150 people died from lack of proper food and medical attention.

The three years that followed were an unrelenting hell for Dakota people. Conditions at Crow Creek were so harsh that three hundred people died within the first few months. Families survived on a soup made of rancid meat and cooked in a trough built of green wood. They lacked adequate clothing for the winter, sufficient food for themselves or their children, or any means of surviving in an arid, drought-prone land far from their traditional foods and medicines. Missionary Williamson reported in 1864 that his students were mostly older, adding, "Nearly all the small children died in 1863." In March 1864, G. W. Knox, former superintendent of schools, wrote, "Over 600 children alone died while I was there with them owing to a lack of vegetables and wild fruit."

On each March, we grieved for all those who had suffered, placing a stake at each mile with the names of two of the original marchers. We mourned the relatives who had died during the March, those who had suffered from cold and hunger, and those who would later die from disease and malnutrition. Each stake we placed carried the name of an adult who had been the head of the household. Implicit in our prayers was the fate of the children.

As I looked around the room at the Henderson center, it was the presence of the children among us that bore witness to the devotion of Dakota people to their families, who regarded their children as "beloved," as sacred beings. There was, perhaps, no greater loss to the Dakota people than depriving them of their ability to raise and protect their children. Far greater even than the loss of the land, or the relentless coercion to surrender cultural traditions, the deaths of so many children was an act of heartless cruelty, a bloodstain on Minnesota's history that cannot be removed.

On each March, we follow the same footsteps as our ancestors, over and again as many times as we will need to heal from the past. On this third March, we had begun to carry many children with us and to hold their well-being as a responsibility shared by all of us. Children are now safe to run and play because someone will always look out for them. In this way, we retrace our ancestors' footsteps with a new March, where the children have plenty of warm food and a safe place to sleep and are surrounded by loving relatives. We heal this way, by replacing the horror with children who are beloved once again.

This story, however, presents a much different perspective on history from the story that continues to be taught in our public schools. A painting by John Gast in 1872 called *American Progress* shows the inexorable westward march of the settlers, led by a white-robed Columbia holding a schoolbook and stringing telegraph wire. In stark contrast to this vision is the image of Indians and wild animals fleeing. This allegorical painting is symbolic of what has been taught in schoolbooks over the past 150 years, a version of history that rarely considers what happened to these Dakota children, instead burying them beneath a layer of silence as if they never existed. And then we wonder why Native people can't get over the past or why they react with so much anger.

When you look beyond the simplistic rationalizations that have been taught in schools and follow this story back down to its root, to the family, to the children who were meant to be kept safe and were not, then it becomes an experience that is devastating to any human being. Even in times of war, our shared humanity dictates that children be spared from grievances between countries, between governments. When hundreds of children die from disease and starvation because they were Indian, this is a crime against humanity that cannot be forgotten. This is the version of history that has been left for Native people to carry and remember.

When that student asked me about anger in that sentence in my book, I did not say all of this. Instead, I said to her, "Imagine if it was your own mother or your grandmother . . ."

And then came the boarding schools. As historian David Wallace Adams states in *Education for Extinction,* the last "Indian War" was fought against Native children:

For tribal elders who had witnessed the catastrophic developments of the nineteenth century—the bloody warfare, the near extinction of the bison, the scourge of disease and starvation, the shrinking of the tribal base, the indignities of reservation life, the invasion of missionaries and white settlers—there seemed to be no end to the cruelties perpetrated by whites. And after all this, the schools. After all this, the white man had concluded that the only way to save Indians was to destroy them, that the last great Indian war should be waged against children. They were coming for the children.

In 1879, while Dakota people were still struggling to recover from another removal to the Santee Reservation in Nebraska, the first federal boarding school was established. In the effort to end Native control of their land, governmental decision makers generally followed two policies: physical extermination and cultural genocide, also referred to as "civilizing" Indians. Carl Schurz, a former Commissioner of Indian Affairs, was actually considered a humanitarian when he argued for the latter in 1881: "We are told that it costs little less than a million of dollars to kill an Indian in war. It costs about one hundred and fifty dollars a year to educate one at Hampton or Carlisle. If the education of Indian children saves the country only one small Indian war in the future, it will save money enough to sustain ten schools like Carlisle, with three hundred pupils each, for ten years. To make a liberal appropriation for such a purpose would, therefore, not only be a philanthropic act, but also the truest and wisest economy."

Two years earlier, Captain Richard H. Pratt had been given permission to establish the first off-reservation boarding school for Native children. Modeled on a prison school he developed in Florida, the Carlisle Indian Industrial School in Carlisle, Pennsylvania, launched the beginning of the boarding school system for Native children across the country. Considered a friend of Native people by virtue of not supporting extermination, Pratt was convinced that a system of total immersion in white culture was essential to severing the ties between Native children and their communities. "A great general has said that the only good Indian is a dead one, and that high sanction of his destruction has been an enormous factor in promoting Indian massacres. In a sense, I agree with the sentiment, but only in this: that all the Indian there is in the race should be dead. Kill the Indian in him, and save the man," Pratt said.

Within the next three decades, nearly five hundred schools were established across the United States, with churches running 460 government-funded boarding and day schools. In 1891, the Indian Appropriations Act required all Native children to attend school and authorized the Bureau of Indian Affairs to withhold federal rations and payments from any family who refused to send their children to school. This policy remained in place until 1978. More than one hundred thousand Native children were forced by the government to attend these schools. Among these children were my grandparents; my great aunt, who attended Carlisle; my aunts, four of whom grew up in St. Francis Mission School on the Rosebud Reservation; and my mother, who attended Holy Rosary Mission School at Pine Ridge.

When children arrived, many after being abducted from their homes, their hair was cut, their traditional clothing was replaced with uniforms, and they were forced to worship as Christians. Native languages were forbidden, and for that reason many languages are now at risk of disappearing. Thousands of children died from starvation and disease. The cemetery at Haskell Indian School in Lawrence, Kansas, holds 102 student graves, while at least five hundred students were buried elsewhere. Others endured widespread physical and sexual abuse, which continued until the end of the 1980s, as the Bureau of Indian Affairs (BIA) failed to investigate reports of abuse. A 2004 study by the Bureau of Justice Statistics reports that Native women are twice as likely to experience sexual assault than any other ethnic group in the United States. Alcoholism rates are six times greater.

Lakota journalist and boarding school survivor Tim Giago writes,

> My eight year old sister, along with dozens of Lakota girls the same age, was raped at the mission school by a pedophile . . . She told me about her abuse on her deathbed and I, along with her three children, finally understood

why she had become a violent, alcoholic woman for so much of her life . . .
Many of the problems of alcoholism and drug abuse now prevalent in
Indian country can be traced back to the physical, emotional and sexual
abuse suffered at the hands of our keepers in the BIA and mission boarding
schools.

Because the United States has yet to acknowledge the harms inflicted
through this educational system, the Boarding School Healing Project
was created to document the abuse and show its connection to high rates
of violence, addiction, and sexual abuse. Sammy Toineeta, Lakota, who
helped found the Boarding School Healing Project, said, "It is one of the
grossest human rights violations because it targeted children and was the
tool for perpetrating cultural genocide."

A 2003 report, "American Indian Children in Foster Care," estimates
that one-half of all Native people were either raised in boarding schools or
parented by adults raised in boarding schools. As generations of Native
children grew up separated from their families, tribes, and cultural traditions, they never learned what it meant to be part of a traditional Native
family or any family at all. They were unprepared to teach their own children when they began to have families. Social workers evaluated Native
families based on white cultural values and removed Native children at
drastic rates that far exceeded any other cultural group. In the late 1960s,
more than 25 percent of all Native children were placed in foster homes,
adoptive homes, or institutions. In 1969, sixteen states reported that 85
percent of the Native children in foster care were not living with Native
families.

Here in Minnesota, where we take pride in our reputation as a good state
to raise families, the rate of removing Native children from their homes for
adoption into white families was among the highest in the nation. In 1974,
one in every eight Native children in Minnesota was living in an adoptive
home. Native children were placed in foster care or adoption at a rate *five
times greater* than non-Native children. William Byler, executive director
for the Association on American Indian Affairs, Inc., wrote, "Ironically,

tribes that were forced onto reservations at gunpoint and prohibited from leaving without a permit, are now being told that they live in a place unfit for raising their children."

By 1978, removing Native children to white foster homes had become such an overused and abused practice that Congress was forced to pass the Indian Child Welfare Act (ICWA). ICWA made it mandatory for foster care agencies to prioritize placing Native children with family members and to follow specific protocol in working with tribes. With this legislation, Congress finally recognized the impact that this discriminatory practice had on Native tribes and their children.

Native families suffered another blow in the 1960s and '70s when the Indian Health Service sterilized an estimated twenty-five thousand Native women and girls without their consent, and sometimes without their knowledge, during other surgeries. Native women experience the highest rate of violence of any group in this country, a situation that dates back to at least the 1862 Dakota War and the practice of soldiers physically abusing vulnerable Native women. Cherokee activist Andrea Smith argues in her book *Conquest: Sexual Violence and American Indian Genocide* that in order to take Native land, Europeans used sexual assault against Native women as a way of destroying the traditional social structure of Native communities, where violence against women was rare. According to the Department of Justice, 70 percent of sexual violence on Native women today is committed by non-Natives.

Many Native people suffer from the long-term effects of these policies, including feeling a sense of shame simply for being Native. Despite the stories, the documentation, and even the statistics, Native people have yet to receive acknowledgment for these harms.

No one wants to believe that they or their ancestors are capable of such cruelty. A careful reading of the United Nations' definition of genocide brings undeniable clarity: "acts committed with intent to destroy, in whole or in part, a national, ethnical, racial or religious group, as such: a) killing members of the group; b) causing serious bodily or mental harm to the group; c) deliberately inflicting on the group conditions of life calculated to bring about its physical destruction in whole or in part; d) imposing measures intended to prevent births within the group; e) forcibly transferring the children of one group to another group." We have failed as a country, and as the state of Minnesota, to recognize the genocidal policies and atrocities that have been committed against Native people.

Again, I ask, imagine if this happened to your child or your grandchild . . .

Timeline

1491 An estimated fifteen million Native people inhabit North America, having established sophisticated tribal societies whose contributions to pharmacology, art, government, architecture, science, and ecology remain largely unacknowledged in our contemporary education system.

1492 Native people discover an uninvited guest on this land, Christopher Columbus.

1830 **Indian Removal Act**—signed by Andrew Jackson, authorizes the president to negotiate with Native tribes to exchange their lands east of the Mississippi River for lands west of the river.
1836—Creek people removed from homeland
1838—Cherokee Trail of Tears

1862 **U.S.–Dakota War,** followed by the removal of Dakota people from Minnesota and abrogation of all treaties.

1879 **Carlisle Indian Industrial School** established as the model for the boarding school system.

1883 **Indian Religious Crimes Code**—prohibits Native ceremonies under risk of imprisonment.

1887 **General Allotment (Dawes) Act**—allots tribal lands held in common to Native individuals.

1891 **Indian Appropriations Act**—requires all Native children to
      attend school and authorizes the BIA to withhold federal rations
      from any family who refuses; policy continues until passage of the
      Indian Child Welfare Act in 1978.

1898 **The Curtis Act**—reaffirms allotment of tribal lands on
      reservations and ends tribal sovereignty in the territories.

1906 **An Act for the Preservation of American Antiquities**—
      makes excavation or theft of historic ruins or objects of antiquity
      on federal lands a criminal offense; Native remains and artifacts
      are defined as "archaeological resources" and considered federal
      property.

1924 **Indian Citizenship Act**—gives U.S. citizenship to Native people,
      including the right to vote; does not provide full protection under
      the Bill of Rights to Natives living under tribal governments.

1934 **Indian Reorganization Act**—or Wheeler-Howard Act, ends
      land allotment, reinstitutes the role of sovereign tribes as
      governments for Native people, and restores tribal lands and
      powers.

1952 **Voluntary Relocation Program**—provides vocational training
      and assistance for reservation Natives to relocate to designated
      urban areas; designed as part of the federal government's
      termination of responsibility for Native welfare.

1953 **Termination Resolution**—terminates federal-Indian trust
      relationship; between 1954 and 1962, Congress terminates trust
      relationship with sixty-one tribes.

1968 **Indian Civil Rights Act**—prohibits tribal governments from
      enacting or enforcing laws that violate individual rights.

1970 **President Nixon's Special Message on Indian Affairs**—sets a
      new direction for national policy: self-determination for Native
      tribes.

1972 **Indian Education Act**—guarantees future generations of Native Americans the tools necessary to compete in modern society without necessitating the abandonment of Native culture and practices.

1975 **Indian Self-Determination and Education Assistance Act**—reverses efforts at termination and gives tribes greater control over funding.

1978 **American Indian Religious Freedom Act**—protects the right of Native people to participate in traditional religions, including access to sacred sites, possession of sacred objects, and worship through traditional ceremonies.

1978 **Indian Child Welfare Act**—protects the best interests of Indian children and promotes the stability and security of Indian tribes and families.

1990 **Native American Graves Protection and Repatriation Act**—protects Native rights to remains, funerary objects, and cultural items; requires federal agencies and museums to provide information and repatriation of Native cultural items to tribes.

2007 **United Nations Declaration on the Rights of Indigenous Peoples**—recognizes the rights of indigenous peoples, including self-determination.

2010 **Tribal Law and Order Act**—strengthens tribal law enforcement, especially in areas relating to domestic and sexual violence; improves programs to treat substance abuse and those for at-risk youth.

Danielle, Harley, Emma, and Sue Eagle

Harley and Sue Eagle

I first met Harley and Sue Eagle at the 2006 Dakota Commemorative March. They drove down from Canada in a station wagon piled high with suitcases, the faces of their two young daughters, Danielle and Emma, watching from the back windows with wide, curious eyes. In the gymnasium at the Lower Sioux Community Center, where we would sleep that night, they quietly set up a small family circle, dragging foam mattresses, unrolling sleeping bags, and unpacking books along with pajamas.

In the morning, we woke before the sun came up, dressed quickly in the dark, and made our way to the prayer circle outside. A layer of frost covered the long grass with a white iridescence that glowed in the first rays of sunlight. After the prayer, with our breath rising like mist in the cold November air, we began to walk. The lead car rolled at three miles an hour, emergency lights flashing, its trunk full of wood stakes tied with red prayer ties. Phyllis Roberts, the elder who carried the *canupa,* the pipe, walked in white canvas tennis shoes and a long black skirt. She told us the canupa needed a space kept open behind her. Several steps back, a young Dakota woman followed Phyllis, carrying a staff with thirty-eight eagle feathers in honor of the thirty-eight warriors who were hanged at Mankato in 1862.

Sometimes the men would forget that this March was organized and led by Dakota women. They would take charge of the eagle staffs, setting a fast pace that pressed too close to the canupa. They too were healing, remembering in their bodies how it must have felt to be separated from their wives and children after the 1862 war, how they could not protect them from what came afterward. So they tried to lead the group, pouring their own grief into movement, into action. In the long days of walking, patience and compassion were the rule. But on the last day, the seventh day, after walking nearly 150 miles, the men were asked to move to the back of the group. The women, once more, would lead this *unsica*, pitiful, group of survivors to the concentration camp that waited for them at the edge of the Mississippi River below Fort Snelling.

While Sue drove their car in the long caravan that followed the marchers, Harley walked quietly with his daughters near the back of the group, maintaining a respectful distance well behind the canupa. He answered Emma's questions with patient good humor, sometimes leaning down to listen to Danielle's softly spoken words. Often they simply walked in companionable silence, feeling the presence of prayer that comes with walking. When we stopped at each mile marker to place a wood stake in the ground, offering prayers and tobacco to the original marchers whose names were written on each side in Dakota, Emma and Danielle stood in line with Harley and Sue. When they grew tired of walking, they rode with Sue. She drove cheerfully, one foot riding the brake, as we walked from sunrise until an hour before sunset.

While the younger kids ran through the ditch alongside the road, laughing and playing, forgetting where they were, Danielle and Emma stayed close to their parents. They watched as people wept, sometimes overcome with grief as they recognized the name of a relative on a stake. They listened at night when we talked in circle, sharing our thoughts and feelings.

One morning, I walked several miles with Harley, talking about the challenges of healing from trauma like that experienced on the original march. It was Harley who first told me of the ceremony of the child-beloved described in Ella Deloria's novel of pre-contact Dakota life, *Waterlily*. The reason why we lived as we did as the *Oceti Sakowin Oyate*, Harley said, was to raise beloved children.

Later, our small group stood near the side of a gravel road that followed the course of the Minnesota River, a wide, slow water visible through the cottonwoods and oak trees that lined its banks. We could hear the sharp bray of a pheasant in the woods and the sudden rustle in the underbrush as a rabbit scurried out of sight. We could smell wood smoke drifting lazily on the breeze that reddened cheeks as we waited. It was a beautiful day, one that evoked the words spoken by Clifford Canku, a spiritual leader from Sisseton who traveled with us, who said, "Your relatives want you to be happy. All this suffering they went through, it's so that you could live and be happy."

As we waited, the thin, high voice of a woman began to sing a prayer song as another woman pounded a wood stake in the ground. It was a poignant moment when the names were read out loud in Dakota by an elder. We heard the old names once more, listened as they were lifted on the wind and echoed through the trees, remembered, an honoring as simple and eloquent as unspoken grief can be.

As the elder spoke each name, I thought of Harley's words. When we mourned our relatives on this walk, we simply included their children in our prayers. I tried to think of my own children and grandchildren, of what it would mean to have walked with them in 1862, to be unable to protect them, to know that they were suffering, to listen to my grandson cry or, worse, to know the meaning of his silence. I could not do it. I could not allow myself to imagine how that felt. It was clear to me in that moment that we have not yet begun to open our hearts to the full enormity of what had been done to these children. It was too big, too dark, too rapacious, to open up to all at once. The deaths of so many children were an act of heartless cruelty that haunts us all, whether we recognize it or not.

Nearly three years later, I flew to Winnipeg to visit the Eagle family. Although I did not know them well, the time spent on the March had forged a kinship among all of us. I knew that Harley was Dakota/Salteaux First Nations, enrolled in the Wapaha Ska (White Cap) Dakota First Nations Reserve in Saskatchewan, Canada, while Sue was Russian Mennonite, raised in Ontario, the southernmost tip of Canada. "On stolen land," Harley would later add, while Sue's expression did not change; the truth holds no fear for her. They share a position as co-coordinators of indigenous work for the Mennonite Central Committee in Canada, the service arm of the Mennonite Church. They also homeschool their two daughters.

I first became interested in talking with Harley after learning about his work with restorative justice, a process that emphasizes repairing the harm caused by a crime with the intention of preserving a just, peaceful society. As I came to know the Eagle family, I realized that Harley's work went much deeper as part of a collaboration with his wife, Sue, that included his daughters as well. For the Eagle family, healing begins at home. As a family, they have committed their considerable energy and talents to creating a new vision for living in, and changing, a colonized world. It was their shared commitment to creating an intentional, mindful family collaboration, as well as their eloquence in speaking about their work, that drew me here.

I came with questions: How did Harley, as a Dakota man, reconcile his work within the Mennonite Church? How did homeschooling their children begin to undo the patterns established in the Native community through generations of children raised in residential schools? And finally, the question I posed to each person I interviewed: How do we heal from historical trauma and raise beloved children?

Arriving in Winnipeg in early May, I saw first the immense spread of a flooded river from my airplane window, the surreal image of tiny houses perched in the middle of a large lake. The Red River, which had done so much damage in Fargo, North Dakota, had continued to wreak havoc as its spring-swollen waters flowed north. Yet the city of Winnipeg—a bustling trade town of seven hundred thousand with the largest Native population in Canada—was relatively untouched, protected by a massive diversion project.

When I stepped out of the elevator at my hotel and looked around for the Eagles, at first all I saw were people wearing suits and party dresses and big hair, an incongruous image for this modest lodging. Then, off to the side, a beautiful sight: all four Eagles standing quietly in a row, as if forming their own reception line, wearing jeans and jackets, and smiling their welcome. I hugged each one in turn, beginning with Harley; then Danielle, now ten, her face shadowed by the hat she wore pulled low over her eyes;

Sue, warm and inviting even though she had just stepped off a plane that same afternoon; and Emma, at eight, funny and playful, bearing a strong resemblance to her older sister.

As we lingered over dinner at a restaurant that evening, I offered small gifts to the family: wild rice, chokecherry syrup, books and markers for the girls. I sat opposite Danielle, the eldest daughter, who as yet had barely spoken a word. When the conversation turned to cats, suddenly she burst forth with a story that had me laughing every time I thought of it. Their cat, Midnight, evidently not too bright, had managed to fall behind the piano and cried piteously until rescued. While feeling bad for the cat, I admired the energy and ease with which Danielle told her story, revealing her shyness as partly a choice about where and when she would speak. When she finished her story, she turned to her mother and asked in a pleading voice, "Can I have a puppy?" Sue said no and smiled, this evidently being a question that was repeated often.

Betraying no sign of her own travel fatigue, Sue sat contentedly between her daughters, juggling the conversation, her daughters' questions, and ordering the meal, seemingly without effort. While they entertained me, Harley's family waited at their home, having arrived early that week for a visit. Yet they showed no signs of feeling pressured or rushed. At the other end of the table, Emma persuaded Harley to turn his hat sideways and stroke his chin as if deep in thought. She stepped back to judge the effect, smiling to herself.

At forty, Harley is still a young man, his long ponytail showing few signs of gray. With his hat turned sideways, his calm intelligence and thoughtfulness were softened by the playful humor he shared with his daughters. While he seems a natural fit for leading circle work, Harley's path has required a great deal of personal reflection and transformation, a process that began when he met Sue.

Growing up with his family on the White Cap Reserve, Harley was unaware of the history that connected the Dakota with their homeland in Minnesota or the diaspora that carried them to Canada after the 1862

Dakota War. In 1973, when Harley was eight, his family visited Wounded Knee just months after the AIM occupation made headlines across the country. A few years later, his parents became born-again Christians and no longer participated in Native ceremonies and traditions, turning completely away from their Native identity. Harley grew up knowing only the bare facts of his history: that his great-grandfather was Red Eagle and his great-grandfather's wife was the daughter of White Cap, a Dakota leader who fled to Canada after the 1862 war. Harley's mother, who is Anishinaabe, spent a year at a residential school before her father fought with the government to send her to a girls' school with more liberal funding. Like many of her generation, like my own mother, she has struggled to acknowledge her identity.

After graduating from high school in Port Hardy on Vancouver Island in the late 1980s, Harley followed his father's footsteps into work at a pulp mill as a chip tender. He was a regular guy, dating women who were attracted to his dark good looks and playing "Bad, Bad Leroy Brown" on the piano. It was his love of music that drew him to join a community choir made up of people of all ages, ethnic backgrounds, and musical abilities. There he met Sue, a fair-skinned farmer's daughter, who was working on an assignment for the Mennonite Church.

When Harley realized by Sue's manner and comments in the choir that she was not going to put up with disrespectful behavior, he quickly became a perfect suitor. This was a turning point for Harley, the moment in which he had to choose between the life in which he was raised, with its conventional views of women, and the direction that Sue's self-respect seemed to suggest, that there was another way to walk in this world.

"I think that it was something that I wanted at my core," Harley said. "That was me recognizing here's another human being who is striving to be a true and authentic human being. I was attracted to that. I also know it scared the heck out of most guys. It's very intimidating to those of us men who have been trained in that way of being a man in this society."

Or rather, of being a man raised in a society in which gender roles have been defined by European values rather than the more equitable roles that men and women played in traditional Dakota society. While men were responsible for hunting and protecting the family, women raised the children and were in charge of the home. Women were held in high regard for their abilities to create and nurture new life. The crucial difference was that both roles were considered equally valuable to their society. The shift in attitudes toward women was one of the consequences of assimilation, of adopting European cultural values.

By choosing a partner who challenged him to see his own underlying patterns of behavior and thought, Harley took the first step toward the work that he and Sue would eventually share, a lifetime of returning to "authentic relationship" with each other, with their children, and with their community.

"It's about restoring a relationship that's based on love and respect," Harley said. "I realize that I have to go through that process and will continue going through that process until the day I die because of what has been undone, not just in my own life, but also in my ancestors' lives. I have to learn again what it means to be in love with a woman, and then with women in general, because of how I've been socialized as a male in this society. I will have to continue learning that and falling in love for the rest of my life because of what I've lost. With children, too. I need to be in authentic relationship with children."

Part of what has been lost is the kinship system that once guided indigenous people in their relationships with one another. "Exacting and unrelenting obedience to kinship demands made the Dakotas a most kind, unselfish people, always acutely aware of those about them and innately courteous," Ella Deloria wrote, describing Dakota people before contact with Europeans so greatly influenced the culture. Children learned from an early age the proper way of behaving toward each person in their lives, a practice that engaged them early in respectful behavior. When European settlers forced Native people to accept a new system of language, traditions, and values in order to absorb them into a European-based culture, that was the beginning of "colonization" and the end of civilized living as defined by Native people.

"For myself as a man, I'm taught that I am the figure of authority in the family and that everyone else in the family is below me," Harley said. "Women are inferior to me, and I am better than my children. I think all of these ideas have been created to keep us separate, to reestablish a different order in society that's about power and control."

The idea that men were the head of the household has its roots in some of the early Christian teachings—texts that Sue said have been misinterpreted and taken out of context.

"'As Christ is the head of the church, so is the man the head of the family,'" Sue said. "Lots of people actually believe that. Well, what did Christ do? Christ risked everything to stand up to government, he stood up to authority, went against all the cultural norms, spent time with women, respected women. But Christianity teaches that out of context. You think about Christ being the head of the church and you start thinking of him as the king. You pull it away from what it truly was, and then you start saying man's authority is the ultimate, and women must be submissive."

"So authentic relationship becomes about undoing all of that," Harley said. "It becomes about putting myself in a position where I realize that I am not the head of the house. In our Dakota traditions, the lodge is the women's lodge. We as men need to behave appropriately in order to stay."

"So I don't put your stuff outside and you get humiliated by the rest of the community because they know you did something wrong," Sue noted, a teasing smile on her face.

The first step, Harley explained, is seeing how we're raised inside of a culture that emphasizes conformity and behaving according to certain rules so that the system of wealth and power can be maintained. Our schools teach language, history, science, and mathematics from a single point of view while insisting that this knowledge is the standard for measuring all others. Yet this knowledge that we've accumulated, the worldview that we teach in our schools, is but one paradigm in a world full of diverse ways of thinking. Imagine the concept of Manifest Destiny, for example, taught from an indigenous perspective.

⌐

After meeting at the community choir on Vancouver Island and becoming the first members to get married, Sue and Harley began working together in 1996 with the SuAnne Big Crow Boys and Girls Club of America on the Pine Ridge Reservation. Living with the Oglala, one of the seven bands of Lakota, Harley returned to Lakota culture and ceremony, facing the fears that he had learned from his family. He discovered that despite his family's silence around their culture, he had been raised following the same protocol and values as the people he met at Pine Ridge.

In their work with Lakota youth, Sue brought education and training in social work and the ability to deal with issues that ranged from physical abuse to building self-esteem. While not academically trained, Harley soon demonstrated his innate skill at working with kids.

"Harley is amazing," Sue said. "The kids all loved him. It's the non-intrusive, non-directive way that he has."

At Pine Ridge, they became involved in restorative justice, a process of resolving harms and differences between people by bringing victims and offenders together. When he first heard of this process through the Mennonites, Harley thought it was crazy. Criminals need to be punished, and the system is responsible for making sure that they are. Learning more about the history of the Oceti Sakowin Oyate while observing how talking circles were being used to deal with difficult issues, Harley began to see that restorative justice uses techniques based on an indigenous worldview. Talking circles also worked well with his natural abilities as a mediator, a role he had always played with his family and friends.

As circle facilitators, Harley and Sue make sure that people are safe within the circle, which offers each person an uninterrupted time to speak. While a simple concept, circle work can have a profound impact on those who participate. Through this work, Harley and Sue help people "get back to basics" by developing the skills needed to communicate as authentic human beings, speaking and listening from the heart rather than the mind and encouraging people to become more self-reflective.

"It's things like learning how to listen respectfully, learning how to talk respectfully, learning how to be with others in respectful ways," Harley explained. "The circle process helps us establish those basic skills that we need."

"We call that competencies," Sue said. "How do we become competent listeners and speakers? Speaking in a respectful way, not taking up all the time, paying attention to who's present. Speaking in ways that take into account who's not there. These are the rules of the circle. Don't try to change somebody else's idea; let them have it."

Getting back to basics also reminds us to reconnect with traditions and the sacred ceremonies that are at the heart of Dakota culture. These ceremonies, which require specific protocol and training to participate, reinforce essential cultural values and help individuals maintain spiritual and emotional balance. The ceremonies include the sacred pipe ceremony; the sweat lodge; vision quest; the Sundance; making of relatives (hunka); girls' rite of passage; and tossing the ball. While specific values vary from tribe to tribe, they remain similar in encouraging a commitment to supporting the community and ensuring the survival of the people. Joseph M. Marshall, a Lakota first language speaker and writer, and founder of Sinte Gleska University on the Rosebud Reservation, lists Lakota values as including humility, perseverance, respect, honor, love, sacrifice, truth, compassion, bravery, fortitude, generosity, and wisdom.

Coercive education through boarding schools and continual pressure to convert to Christianity forced indigenous people to absorb new values that taught a far different relationship between people and ultimately with the earth. While the values listed above are cherished at the heart of religious thought across cultures, Western Europeans taught different perspectives on gender roles, acquiring material goods, and owning land. They also emphasized the needs of the individual versus those of the community. Each of these shifts, and especially the belief that the earth is a resource as opposed to a living, sacred being, has had a devastating impact on Native people.

"The essence of those ceremonies was to help us remember as human beings a certain value, whether it be courage or generosity or humility," Harley said. "What I mean about reconnecting with traditions is reconnecting with the values. When I work with people using the circle, there are values and guidelines that we use within the circle that reinforce the values that help us to be at our best as human beings. We need to be at our best to work with these issues. But we tend to forget as human beings, so we need these kinds of ritual ceremonies to help remind us. That's what I was saying about the process of colonization. It wasn't just about subjugating the people and taking the land; it was about also changing the worldview of the people so that they could be more easily controlled by the system. Our way back is by once again practicing the processes that help us to remember in a really practical way how these values work and how they are efficient, how they are about equality and fairness and remembering and respect."

Hardly the qualities that are portrayed in the media, where Native peoples continue to suffer from stereotypes that serve only to reinforce the image of primitive, noble savages and the inexorable necessity of "civilization." The real story—genocide, ethnic cleansing, and the sheer waste of knowledge attained by a sophisticated culture—is much harder to accept. These stereotypes are no accident, however, as they often serve a purpose in maintaining the myth of the superiority of the invaders.

Challenging the negative portrayals of American Indians in the media and in our schools requires seeing beyond the statistics that too often define Native people in terms of contemporary challenges. Rather than using negative, victim-based terminology that portrays Native people standing in the shadow of mainstream society, we could turn in a new direction. As Severt Young Bear, founder and lead singer of the Porcupine Singers, a traditional Lakota drum group, wrote, we can move from the "darkness," where Native people have forgotten their language and traditional knowledge, to "stand in the light," where we return to an understanding of what Native culture truly means.

"There's so much genius and brilliance within the Native worldview, within Native communities, and within Native people," Harley said. "Sometimes it's hard to see, and sometimes we're told not to believe it because of things we've been taught. Christianity has done a good job of instilling belief in a myth that all things connected to Native spirituality are evil or wrong. We really have to work hard at being who we are as Native people and try to maintain that worldview. A lot of those ways are based on things like respect and courage and humility, those values that I think all of us hope to obtain and live by."

When I asked Sue and Harley about their work with the Mennonite Central Committee (MCC), the service arm of the Mennonite Church, Harley offered a story to help illustrate what they do. At a board meeting where a number of projects were being introduced in a PowerPoint presentation, the image that came up for them was a picture of their entire family. "That is at the root of the way that we see our work," Harley said. "It's about building relationships and seeing what comes out of those relationships."

In particular, they pay attention to people who have historically been overlooked, especially indigenous or, using the term common in Canada, aboriginal women and children. As in the United States, by the 1950s the aboriginal family system had been decimated as generations of children grew up in the institutionalized, and often abusive, environment of residential or boarding schools. When these children became adults and began raising families, many of them lacked parenting skills. Most suffered from cultural confusion and loss of self-esteem. Many more had been victimized by physical and sexual abuse.

In 1951, the Indian Act was changed so that Canadian authorities assumed responsibility for the welfare of Indian children. Within a decade, the social welfare system had become far more aggressive about removing aboriginal children from their homes and placing them in non-Native families. Social workers often failed to understand Native values or the role of the extended family in raising children. Within the Dakota *tiyospaye*, or extended family, for example, a child may have many relatives who share the responsibility for his or her well-being. As Ella Deloria wrote in *Speaking of Indians*, "A woman who had to leave her children behind to go on a journey went with an easy conscience. She knew that her several 'sisters' and the rest would never let a child be abused or allowed to stray off or go hungry . . . As for the child, you can see what it did for him to have so many persons responsible for him. It gave him multiple protection. It insured for him the care that is due all helpless children, even when their own parents might not be there. It was a very comfortable and safe feeling for a growing child."

Instead, in Canada, as in the United States, social workers applied middle-class white values as the standard for judging what a "good home" and "family" should look like. Poverty, poor housing, lack of plumbing, and overcrowding were often cited as grounds for starting custody proceedings, often without evidence that any of these conditions actually constituted child neglect. This era became known as the "Sixties Scoop," as thousands of children were adopted out to white families in the United States and around the world.

Canadian Justice Edwin C. Kimelman concluded in his 1985 investigative report on exporting Native children, "Cultural genocide has been taking place in a systematic routine manner. One gets an image of children stacked in foster homes as used cars are stacked on corner lots, just waiting for the right 'buyer' to stroll by."

Another group that Harley and Sue support is Sisters in Spirit, which honors and remembers aboriginal women who are missing or murdered and whose cases have not been addressed appropriately or been solved. Working together, Sue and Harley support individuals and organizations on a national level, raising awareness of the issues and participating in grassroots events, such as the Sisters in Spirit March to honor missing women.

Recently the Eagles have created a website, Myth Perceptions (http:// mythperceptions.ca), that deconstructs "stereotypes, myths and untruths about Indigenous Peoples," from residential schools to aboriginal art. The site includes a statement by Karen Pace and Dionardo Pizaña examining the qualities that are essential to building trust across differences between people, as well as the full text of the United Nations Declaration on the Rights of Indigenous Peoples. Working closely with Native people who helped develop the document, the Eagles are skeptical of the commitment expressed by both Canada and the United States. "We need to be careful as indigenous people not to get wooed," Harley said. "The patterns are still there. It's still the same systems in place."

An essential part of their work continues to be the training they provide in various communities using circles to deal with a range of issues. A commitment to this process helps to develop the ability of individuals to see and change patterns in their lives and to strengthen the qualities needed to engage in authentic relationships, such as a willingness to be challenged. As most of the time in circle is used to listen to each other, the process helps people become more self-reflective and it strengthens their abilities to remain balanced in volatile situations and to sit with "uncomfortableness" as hard issues are discussed.

Yet despite the importance of the efforts that Harley and Sue are involved in with aboriginal people, their most innovative work comes from within their own family. While some people mistakenly label their hard work as "luck," redefining the relationship between work and family and community has required years of commitment to a process that is intuitive, creative, and infused with the intellectual rigor needed to critically analyze the systems that surround us.

After nearly two years of working with the Boys and Girls Club at Pine Ridge, in 1998 Harley and Sue were asked to assume more of a leadership role in developing relationships in aboriginal communities. Challenging the Mennonite Central Committee (MCC) policy of not allowing children in the office, in 2005 Sue and Harley laid down their own set of rules: we are a package, and we're planning to stay home and come into the office when we need to. As Sue explained, "We're trying to decolonize our family first and ourselves," meaning that their work is not a place where they go from nine to five and then leave at the office.

While living at Pine Ridge, Harley and Sue discovered that their work was most effective when they lived closely with the people in the community, paying attention to the politics and the protocol, realizing that sometimes even owning a lawn mower can become political. By listening, getting to know people, and attending meetings, Sue and Harley developed a way of living their work in which their family was an integral part. When they moved to Winnipeg, they chose to live in a diverse inner-city neighborhood even though it meant sometimes encountering streetwalkers or suspected drug dealers. Rather than shield their girls, they talked to them about why people do what they do and how to remain safe.

Given the historical role of Christian churches, I asked Harley about his experience at MCC. He explained that he is able to work with MCC because they are relatively forthright in acknowledging systemic issues of racism and oppressive behaviors, both within the church and in the broader community. "To be in denial about how the church is totally tied up in the process of colonization would be a terrible lie to perpetuate with the people we were working with," Harley said.

Persuading the church to expand the boundaries regarding their work situation also opened up the possibility of engaging in other, more challenging conversations. One of the difficulties in working through issues around colonization is persuading people that they are deeply engaged in that process, no matter how well intentioned they might seem.

"I remember somebody once characterized our organization as being full of broken world thinkers," Harley said. "What he meant is that it's full of people who think that the world is broken 'out there' and that we need to go out there and help them fix it because we have the answers and we have the money. But if you don't realize that your own life, and your own history, and your own way of being in this world are a part of the brokenness, it creates a dynamic of well-intentioned people who don't even realize that they will cause more damage in the end."

Since the early 1800s, "well-intentioned" missionaries have believed they were saving the souls of Native people by converting them to Christianity and then establishing "well-intentioned" residential schools that were supposed to "kill the Indian and save the man." In the 1880s, Canada imported the boarding school model used in the United States and maintained it into the late 1980s. A 2001 report by the Truth Commission into Genocide in Canada documents the responsibility of the Roman Catholic

Church, the United Church of Canada, the Anglican Church of Canada, and the federal government "in the deaths of more than 50,000 Native children in the Canadian residential school system."

On June 11, 2008, Canadian Prime Minister Stephen Harper apologized to aboriginal peoples for the harms they experienced at residential schools. This statement offers a sharp contrast to the United States, where acknowledgment of genocidal policies such as boarding schools has met strong resistance. The Canadian government approved a $2 billion compensation package known as the Common Experience Payment to all surviving residential school students. Accepting the payment would release the government and churches of all further liability except in cases of sexual abuse and some incidents of physical abuse. Afterward, at least two dozen deaths were attributed to receiving the payments, which sometimes triggered the effects of post-traumatic stress disorder and depression, even in those who had done a lot of healing work.

"I don't know what the answer is," Harley said. "In the midst of genocide and land grabs and Dakotas being forced out of Minnesota and coming into Canada, this whole huge story is being funneled down into the residential school experience, which is huge in and of itself. I do know that we need to keep on talking about it because there are voices and ways of thinking about it that are missing. That's why we jump too quickly to a solution. We trusted in the academic world and the legal world—and the whole leadership structure in our aboriginal communities that's been created by the U.S. and Canadian governments—we trusted that to come up with a solution. The solution they came up with was based on money. We used a process that came from colonized thinking and colonized structures. I'm learning, especially as a male, that I've been taught to have a solution and to fix it. I'm learning to say, no, I don't have that, but I do know of some processes that might be helpful. I don't think a political entity like the government can even scratch the surface of what I need as a human being who has suffered loss."

As aboriginal people continue to fight for justice on many fronts, from recovering stolen land to insisting on the value of an indigenous worldview, it's equally important to remember who we are as human beings. Making change does not justify using just any means, Harley said. It does not justify using *wasichu,* white, methods. To be true to ourselves, we need to act according to the core values that are intrinsic to indigenous culture. The challenge is in seeing how to change, how to decolonize ourselves, when we are already colonized. Again, it means returning to the basics of living as an authentic human being, to trust our instincts, our innate curiosity and creativity, to ask why, and to live without shame.

At the root of racism, Harley continued, is a misplaced belief that a certain group of people with specific physical traits believe that they are superior and that their way of doing things is "of God." That belief dictates that other groups are by necessity inferior. When these groups are defined by skin color, creating a false system that arbitrarily categorizes people according to their ethnicity, then we lose the broader understanding of race as applying to the entire human race. The real issue is more about process, about the worldview that defines the way we as human beings relate to each other and to the world around us. Indigenous people from all over the world have created earth-based cultures. Christianity has supported a worldview based on a belief in the superiority of its own doctrine, a belief that has been used to rationalize genocidal methods.

But it's the indigenous worldview that we need to find our way back out of the mess we've created in the world, Harley added. While scientists debate the exact nature and timing of the earth's "tipping point," that moment in time when the destruction we've inflicted will become irreversible and life threatening, it's time we realize that "we've fallen out of love with the earth. It's about restoring a relationship that's based on love and respect. Now I'm realizing how much I'm missing and how much I've lost because I'm not in authentic relationship with the earth. I have to fall in love with the earth again and figure out what that means."

By rediscovering our relationship with the earth, with ceremony, storytelling, and all the other gifts that are necessary to balance ourselves as human beings, we reestablish an indigenous worldview. Without these aspects, our lives become overly focused on survival, on hoarding, with fulfilling our material needs as most important. When people are focused on survival, they lack the time and energy needed to be creative.

Ultimately, Harley explained, when you're involved in anti-racism work, you have to look at the results, not the intentions. Results need to match your intentions for it to be a good strategy. For the Oceti Sakowin Oyate, the intention has always been to raise beloved children.

The next day, we continued our conversation at the library, a place that was deeply loved by both girls. Both Emma and Danielle devour books, and not just storybooks. They share their mother's love of natural science, of books that describe dinosaurs and volcanoes and rain forests. On our short walk to the library, Harley and the girls balanced on a narrow concrete ledge like three kids playing at the park, while Sue talked about their recent experiment of dropping an egg from the window of their learning center. Once a week, they meet with nine other families who are also teaching their children at home, sharing activities like science experiments or putting on a play.

As soon as we entered the building, the girls vanished into their favorite aisles, content to browse and read for the next hour. Danielle came and sat with us when she was done, listening and reading without ever interrupting our conversation. An elder who taught many years in public schools once said that children who are disruptive have not learned their values at home.

When I asked about homeschooling, Sue corrected me, saying that they prefer to call it life learning, or natural learning, or unschooling.

"I worked in schools as a school counselor before we were married," Sue said. "I saw aboriginal children being 'streamed,' a lot of assumptions being made. Even the smartest ones would get streamed. Government funding does that. I saw children getting lost once they got into high school. I saw the racism in the community, the way people talked. I didn't want my children dealing with that. I wanted them to learn who they are, their American history, their geography, their literature that they could identify with."

Public schools often direct students into specific learning "streams" that group together students of similar learning abilities. Aboriginal students are often assumed to have special needs and are put into classes that may not challenge them. Teachers are more likely to consider them unable to handle material given to the majority of students in their grade level. This practice ultimately leads to increased dropout rates and low self-esteem, as youth fail to reach their potential when they are not given the resources they need to succeed.

Instead, Harley and Sue looked to their coworkers at Pine Ridge who were raising two boys in a homeschool environment. Given the history of residential schools and their distrust of public education, they were intrigued by the possibilities presented by teaching their own children.

"We saw these boys as really creative, free thinkers, critical thinkers, and we thought that was just wonderful," Sue explained. "I think because we were so close to so many people who were suffering from the effects of residential schools that we didn't want to participate in any way in that style of education. And when we began to live our lives in a way that involved a critical analysis of the systems that surround us, we began to realize how much of the public school system perpetuates the lies, perpetuates the patterns of oppression. Also, we recognized that many of the lies and patterns that we had internalized but are trying to undo, we learned in school."

Maintaining a constant awareness of these patterns is very much a part of what Sue and Harley consider to be their work, blurring the distinctions between family and job. Rather than confining their core values and beliefs to small containers of time like the workday or attending church on Sundays, they have chosen an indigenous way to live by incorporating those values into their daily lives. They pay attention to the big issues around racism as well as less visible issues, such as remembering that the simple act of turning on a light switch is often connected to the dams that have been built on rivers on indigenous lands.

"The best way to break patterns is to establish new processes," Harley said. "And the best place to do that is within ourselves." By returning to the teachings of the medicine wheel and the circle, they take responsibility for maintaining the balance in their lives and in their communities.

Although their daughters have never attended public school, they are still bombarded with stories and images all around them that reinforce the values and teachings of white culture. Part of this process of unschooling, Harley added, is knowing that their daughters will learn that white males are in power and define the standards by which we live. Unschooling also means unlearning what society teaches them. That's why it's important to find optometrists and doctors and artists who provide examples of people of color who are brilliant, who are succeeding in professional roles.

Harley and Sue's children also learn through experience, through the freedom of being allowed to try things, fall down, and figure out solutions to problems. This ability to be prepared for whatever life throws at you was an essential aspect of being able to adapt to whatever was going to come over the next hill. Our ancestors knew to let children develop skills that would allow them to deal with difficult situations. When we try to fix everything, we lose the opportunity of nurturing both the creativity and the critical thinking abilities of our children. When they learn cause and effect through experience, they develop their own standards based on experiential learning. "Nurturing that kind of critical thinking," Harley said, "is our goal with our children."

Part of the process is letting go of the patterns of education that we have all been taught and allowing a more natural way of learning to occur. "A child's predominant method of communication until the age of ten is play," Sue said. "It's a challenge to slow down your life enough so that when you go to the grocery store, the kids get to see what it's going to cost. We do experiments, we have a microscope, we explore."

Equally important, their children are not put in the position of being the "aboriginal" children within a class or a group. They're not expected to be role models or teach the rest of the group what it means to be aboriginal.

But if there are no tests, no grades to progress through, how do they measure the effectiveness of this approach? How does a parent decide if unschooling is educating their child, in whatever way they choose to evaluate it? "With unschooling," Sue said, reaffirming Harley's comment about anti-racism work, "it's all about results. As a parent, you want to see the results in your children."

The truest test of their success comes from the words and actions of their children. At the learning center where they were working on presenting *The Tempest,* Sue has led sessions on making masks. Emma's mask has feathers hanging from a medicine wheel, peace signs on the cheeks, and a pin that Harley gave her which says "Give Me Some Truth." "When I see that," Sue said, "I get all choked up. She knows a heck of a lot. And that's an eight-year-old."

Danielle keeps a little plastic desk in her room called the Desk of Justice. She collects racist imagery, stuff from protests they've been part of, her little bin of things demonstrating a deep understanding of what injustice means. Twice she's asked her mother to speak to the manager of the local bookstore about books that use racist imagery. Both girls have challenged their gymnastics coaches when they wanted to use a song based on the stereotyped story of Pocahontas. On another occasion, they were asked to shimmy as part of the choreography. They had spent enough time at Pine Ridge to know it was inappropriate for a child to move in a sexual manner. Sue said, "I had to talk to the coaches and very calmly explain that my daughters were raised to be modest with their bodies, and this was something that was not respectful." The coaches quickly took it out of the choreography.

When Danielle briefly attended an alternative kindergarten for aboriginal children, she challenged one of her Native teachers for using the word "Indian," which was a practice started by Europeans, rather than "indigenous" or "aboriginal." Her teacher told this story to Sue with tears in her eyes, telling her how proud she was of Danielle for standing up to her. And she was right.

In listening to Harley and Sue, I began to understand much more clearly how important Sue's role is in their work. Having first met Sue at the Dakota March where she provided support to Harley and the girls, I found it easy to simply look to Harley for the answers to my questions. I assumed that Harley was working in restorative justice while Sue homeschooled their children, an assumption that fit with stereotypical gender roles. With my focus on how Native people heal from trauma, an articulate indigenous man seemed like the ideal person to talk to about those issues. But to truly understand the intent behind their work, I had to challenge my own unacknowledged assumptions about their family relationship. In other words, I had to decolonize my own thinking in order to understand who they are.

By providing support to Harley and their daughters at the Dakota March, Sue was also acknowledging her understanding of her role as a white person at a Dakota event. This was a conscious political choice made within the context of their family that reflected the level of mindful critical thinking they bring to their lives. This process has encouraged Sue to redefine the patterns of thought ingrained by her schooling and upbringing within the dominant society. Like so many women, Sue has also had to challenge cultural norms to find ways to work with men who refused to talk to her. On a profound level, Sue and Harley are committed to the difficult work of actually "walking their talk" around gender equity and decolonization. In their marriage, they personify the understanding that healing requires full participation from both sides—male and female, Dakota and Mennonite—working through painful issues to find balance once again.

To do this work, Sue brings an understanding and commitment to her own heritage that is equal but separate from Harley's identity as a Dakota man. As a descendant of a family with several generations within the Mennonite Church, Sue introduces herself to the Mennonite Central Committee board in a traditional way, reminding them that her father grew up in Ukraine and her grandparents lived through the Russian Revolution. The Mennonite Church was started by a Catholic priest living in the Netherlands, but after persecution it dispersed to Prussia, Russia, and North and South America. Sue's grandparents survived the Russian Revolution but also lost their family's oral history in the process. With her credentials firmly established within the Mennonite tradition, Sue plays a critical liaison role in their work, finding ways to articulate indigenous concepts that make sense within a Mennonite context. Like Harley, Sue has invested years of rigorous self-reflection to come to an understanding of white/aboriginal relationships.

"When I first started working with indigenous folks, the privileged part of me saw the parallels and thought, well, we were persecuted, too," Sue said. "I didn't understand white privilege at the time. I just saw it as *don't get mad at me because my people had problems, too*." Over the years, the unflinching honesty and intelligence that Sue brings to her work have given her rare insight into the politics and dynamics of white privilege, an understanding that has made her an invaluable partner in the work they do as a family.

Despite the terrible events that aboriginal people have experienced, and even with all the grief and trauma, Harley remains grateful that he can still participate in his own culture and return to land that has been important to his family and tribe for generations—unlike Sue, whose family has lost not only the culture her ancestors knew but also their relationship with their homeland back in Europe. When Harley asked Sue how she handles this loss, it took her several years to come up with an answer. Sue finally replied, "I need to figure out how to be a good guest in this land." Had that kind of thinking happened all those years ago when Europeans first arrived, imagine where we might be today.

One of the ways we can deal with our loss is to learn the history of our ancestors, regardless of culture. Despite growing up without learning much about the history that connects Dakota people in Canada with Minnesota, Harley as an adult became interested in reconnecting with his Dakota family history. After learning about the diaspora to Canada following the 1862 Dakota War in Minnesota, Harley and Sue made participating in the Dakota Commemorative March an important event for their entire family.

"At an identity level, it was huge for me to know just a little bit of my history and where my roots are as a people," Harley said. "It's really important for Danielle and Emma to walk with people that they're related to and then join in the remembrance of those who lost their lives. They've heard a lot about oppression and tragedy and massacres and forced removals and relocations, all those things. I think it's really important for them to know on a personal level that these are my roots, this is my story. And to experience that as a family was really important. Something that happened on this last trip [the 2008 Dakota March] was that Sue was looked to by the Dakota women to be an ally in a critical moment. I think it was really important that folks saw that I wasn't just a Dakota man who happens to be married to a white woman."

On the 2008 Dakota Commemorative March, when the dynamics of the mixed group erupted in hurt feelings between Dakota and white marchers, Sue was asked to speak to the group.

"I stood up and talked about why we were there," Sue said. She explained how at a Dakota event, she takes direction from Dakota people and how important it is to see how white privilege works, that we're all tied into a complex history. And how very difficult it is to see and understand the ways in which white people have benefited from that history. In other words, Sue was reminding them how to be a good guest in this land.

While Sue was talking, Emma insisted on sitting alone with Harley and sharing how she felt about what was happening in the group. "She had a lot to say about what she saw and what she understood as right and wrong and how we should interact as human beings," Harley recalled. "She talked about the story of the walk, why we were there, how she felt about the history of the pain, how we as human beings shouldn't be treating each other that way, that we should be loving one another as human beings. It doesn't matter if you're indigenous or white; we need to be loving to one another. I realized it wasn't like I was sitting with a child. It was like I was sitting with an elder."

And there it was, a new beginning in the lives of two children who had already learned at a young age what it means to stand up for themselves, to refuse to allow their culture to be treated as inferior simply because adults have failed to be conscious of their words or actions. In moving beyond the limitations of a society that has not yet learned to look beyond survival, always grasping for the safety that material goods imply, Emma and Danielle have been raised to see themselves as holistic beings, as creative, critical thinkers who see the value of ceremony, storytelling, and traditions. They know their history, these two, and they see the world exactly as it presents itself. What a gift.

But for the thousands of Native people who have endured and lost and struggle still, what we can do is reconnect with the traditions that reconnect us with our values, with an indigenous way of seeing the world. Harley said, "In order to undo some of those things, we need as people of color or Native people, we need to say, no, our ways are not inferior. Our ways and processes are good, and they are based on the rhythms of the universe. People from all over the world use a circle process. Indigenous people from all over the world use earth-based cultures."

As we work toward reestablishing authentic relationships with each other and with our children, we also need to learn again how to fall in love with the earth, Harley said. We need to restore a relationship that's based on love and respect.

"I think her shoulders are big enough to hold our pain," Harley continued. "I think that's always the first disconnect that's imposed, the disconnect from the land. And then it's our children. The residential school process was about taking our children away. And then it's about changing the relationship between man and woman. All of that is designed to keep us disconnected from our own spirits. And from trusting the energy that's within us, that connects us."

Reverend Clifford Canku

Clifford Canku

He leaned back, feeling the cool dampness of the wall through his thin shirt, his long legs stretched before him on the floor. Outside the window that opened high above his head, he could hear the measured cadence of a soldier who called out the changing of the guard. For a precious few minutes he would have peace from the inevitable routines of prison. He began his letter with a pen borrowed from the missionary who visited every few days, using the written words he had learned. The missionary wished him to accept the white man's religion. Before the war, he had laughed, and his brothers had laughed with him . . .

We sat in stunned silence; not a cough, not a whisper broke the utter stillness in the room. On a gray afternoon in late winter, a group of students, Dakota community members, scholars, and historians listened as Clifford Canku read out loud from Dakota letters that were written by prisoners held at Camp McClellan in Davenport, Iowa, after the Dakota War of 1862. As he read each sentence slowly with his distinct Dakota accent, we were hearing the voices of our ancestors.

We sat in the dim light, staring at a magnified image of a man's hand writing on the screen, the faint shape of his words echoing across the years, almost as if he were speaking directly to us. The letters revealed that prisoners were under great pressure to convert to Christianity. Others told harsh stories. "We're very cold, and they took the stove away from us," one prisoner wrote. "A lot of people have died." Another letter told how the guards raped Dakota women who worked at the prison, cleaning and cooking for the prisoners. The men couldn't protect them, so they sang to let them know they were praying for them. Other letters are painful to families because they talk about Dakota men who collaborated with the U.S. Army.

Did the prisoners hear rumors of the suffering at Crow Creek? Perhaps they wrote only to assure their wives and sisters and mothers that they were still alive and to learn whether their families had survived. They may have written to offer courage for the women, to maintain a slender thread of continuity in lives that had been torn apart by a war that was already lost before the first shot was fired. Because they were Indians, the men were punished with prison regardless of their role in the war, and the women and children were treated as less than animals, paying with their health, their dignity, and their lives.

For Clifford, translating these letters is about truth telling, even if they make people uncomfortable.

In spring 1863, about 265 men were shipped to this federal military prison in Iowa, several months after thirty-eight warriors had been hanged at Mankato as punishment for their alleged role in the 1862 Dakota War. A quarter of these prisoners would die before the survivors were finally released three years later. During that time, their only communication with their families at Crow Creek was through letters written to Stephen R. Riggs and John Williamson.

The letters were saved at the Minnesota Historical Society in the papers belonging to Reverend Riggs, a Presbyterian missionary who spent much of his life working with Dakota people. The letters sat untouched for decades until a group of five elders, all first language speakers, began the laborious process of translating each letter. Led by Clifford Canku, at that time a professor at Sisseton Wahpeton College, the original group included William Iron Moccasin, Davis Robertson, Michael Simon, and Hildreth Venegas. "It is rediscovering the history," Clifford said. "It is a living history for us."

In late 2008, Clifford presented the Dakota Letters Project at a conference on the ethnic cleansing of Native people held at Southwest Minnesota

State University. This two-day conference was part of a series called "Difficult Dialogues" that was organized by Dr. Chris Mato Nunpa, associate professor of indigenous nations and Dakota studies at Southwest Minnesota State University. An impressive roster of speakers included Ward Churchill, Waziyatawin Angela Wilson, and Chris Mato Nunpa, who gave powerful, electrifying lectures on the genocide of Dakota people. But it was the simple language of the prisoners' letters that brought home the reality of this conference in a way that no other speech could begin to approach.

Clifford Canku and the elders he worked with understood the power of these letters. They knew how important it was to preserve the voices of our ancestors. As Clifford read, his voice echoed from stockade walls, carrying the silence of men praying and the scratch of a pen moving slowly on rough paper. As he spoke, their words moved from our minds to our bodies, impressing this history on our skin and in our blood. We began to breathe together, sharing a silence that grew heavy with presence.

In many ways, Dr. Reverend Clifford Canku, Sr., has been preparing all his life for the work of translating the prisoners' letters. He was born in 1938 on the Lake Traverse Dakota Reservation in northeastern South Dakota, an enrolled member of the Sisseton-Wahpeton Oyate. His first words as a child were spoken in Dakota, the only language he knew until he learned English when he was six years old.

When I met Clifford in 2002 at the first Dakota Commemorative March, I was intimidated by his graying Mohawk, his status as an elder and spiritual leader, and the way he carried himself as a powerful Dakota warrior even in his middle years. But when he spoke, when his face was creased by a sweet smile, then I knew his kind heart. During the March, Clifford moved quietly through the group each day, checking in with people, offering guidance and direction while listening deeply to what was said. In moments of tension or grief, he knew what to say that would help us move forward. His words never failed to remind us of our better selves and our innate desire to live according to Dakota values.

I walked with Clifford on the last day of the March, shortly after discovering that my relatives were among the original marchers. It was heartbreaking to recognize their names on the stake pounded in the ground at that mile marker. I told Clifford that I felt a powerful sense of grief for the original marchers, that in mourning for my own family, I had felt the March become personal as well for all Dakota people.

Clifford told me that we are all part of the collective unconscious, and the people's connection to it is growing stronger, partly because of events like the March. When people come back to their heritage, he explained, when they learn their language, when they march to reconcile a part of history that has never been acknowledged, they are slowly putting together the pieces of their lives like a puzzle.

Later, as we approached the bridge that would lead us down to Fort Snelling, Clifford moved through the group with a bowl of sage, stopping briefly to allow each woman to draw the smoke into her face, hair, and breath. He was there when we stopped, and he has continued to be present at every event possible that acknowledges this history. With his presence comes a feeling of safety, that while we are traveling in the sanctuary of prayer, nothing will harm us.

One of the marchers—a woman who distrusted Christian churches—said afterward that if she lived near Sisseton where Clifford led services as a Presbyterian minister, she would even go to church.

Beginning with the earliest visits from Jesuit missionary explorers in Wisconsin and Minnesota, the Dakota have had contact with Christian missionaries for over three centuries. The American Board of Commissioners for Foreign Missions authorized the first mission among the Dakota in 1834. Stephen R. Riggs began working with the Dakota in 1837 as a Presbyterian missionary, quickly becoming fluent in the language. He eventually published *Grammar and Dictionary of the Dakota Language* and helped translate the Bible into Dakota. Following the 1862 war, Riggs continued to preach to the prisoners until their release in 1866, gaining many converts during this traumatic period, some of whom may have believed that converting would save them from hanging. His language skills and his long familiarity with the Dakota meant that many of the prisoners turned to him with the letters they wrote to their families.

Through the nineteenth century, each of the major churches—Catholic, Episcopalian, Presbyterian—followed similar mission programs on the reservations. They trained Native ministers to help with converting new members, established schools that served to reinforce white cultural values while instilling religious training, and organized annual convocations to celebrate their accomplishments. In addition to gaining new converts, success was measured by the number of Native people in their congregation who were transformed from hunters in traditional outfits to farmers wearing the clothes of the "western civilization." Along with the promise of salvation, there were undoubtedly pragmatic incentives to convert. Native ministers, priests, and other clergy could provide access to money and influence, thereby reinforcing white cultural values in the name of religion.

As pressure for land continued to build in the late 1800s, efforts to assimilate American Indians also increased. Traditional spiritual beliefs and practices were considered pagan and an obstacle toward the goal of becoming "civilized." In 1883, the Bureau of Indian Affairs implemented laws suppressing traditional Native religious practices, known as the Indian Religious Crimes Code. According to the code, American Indians were not allowed to practice their ceremonies, and medicine men were ordered to stop or risk imprisonment. Access to land or sites that tribes revered as sacred became far more difficult as the land was purchased or confiscated. For nearly one hundred years, Native spiritual practices were criminalized. The freedom to practice their own religion was not returned to Native people until the passage of the American Indian Religious Freedom Act in 1978.

For the Dakota, moving to a reservation in the 1850s limited their access to their sacred place of origin at Bdote, the confluence of the Minnesota and Mississippi rivers. Ironically, the Dakota were imprisoned at a concentration camp on this sacred site following the 1862 Dakota War. An oral history passed down by families has preserved a record that was not kept by the whites: how prisoners were forced to surrender their medicine bundles and sacred items, watching as they were burned in a fire. Further removal to Crow Creek meant that the Dakota lived far from the graves of their ancestors as well as their sacred places at a time when they were forbidden to use their own spiritual practices. For a people whose religious beliefs were deeply enmeshed with every aspect of life and who were suffering tremendous losses, this was devastating.

As a result, Christianity is the predominant religion in several Native communities. Yet many Natives have also maintained their commitment to traditional spiritual beliefs and ceremonies. Like Clifford, an ordained Presbyterian minister, they have found a way to resolve any internal conflict and incorporate both Christianity and traditional beliefs into their spiritual practice.

In 2009, I visited Clifford at Sisseton to learn, among many topics, how he reconciles his work as a Dakota spiritual leader with his work and training in a Christian church. Clifford arranged for us to have lunch with Gabrielle (Gaby) Tateyuskanskan, one of the cofounders of the Dakota Commemorative March; her mother, Yvonne Wynde, an educator; and her sister, Lisa Lopez, a tribal lawyer working with child protection.

After arriving early at the restaurant, Clifford and I sat in his car with the windows open, watching the birds pick through the long grass and weeds that were newly free of snow. While we waited, I flipped through the pages of Clifford's photo albums from his days as a Presbyterian minister. He opened the tiny notebook that he carries and read to me his favorite quote: "It's not what you do but who you are that is important." Over the next two hours, I would have a chance to see this statement in action.

We met at the Crossroads Restaurant, part of Sisseton-Wahpeton's small, Native-owned casino. We walked past the ringing of slot machines, past the empty bingo room, and into a restaurant where the tables were mostly full. After introductions were made, Yvonne said to me without preamble, "So you're writing a book?" I told them the story of the beloved child ceremony in Ella Deloria's book *Waterlily*. Even though we have a list of the original marchers, the names of the children were not recorded anywhere. When hundreds of children died at Crow Creek, I wondered how people survived such loss. How, I asked them, can the Dakota raise beloved children in the midst of so much trauma?

I also asked whether I should even write this book. With so much of this work needing to be done together as people, does it even make sense to reduce these teachings to print? Yvonne turned to Clifford and said we need to define our own terminology and not let the wasichu definitions speak for us. I sensed that this was my answer.

The real challenge, they all agreed, is how to help Native youth survive today. Gaby, who has a daughter in college and a son in high school, tapped my page to make a point: "Youth are still being assaulted today, and we have the highest suicide rate in the country. It's a real challenge for kids to survive. It seems the girls go to college and the boys go to prison." Gaby's son had been harassed by the police and beaten up at school. Lisa's brother, tall for his age, kept a baby seat in his car so he would appear less intimidating when the police pulled him over.

Unfortunately, for many Native families, the legacy of boarding schools is only one example of governmental policies and institutions that for generations have victimized Native people in order to assimilate them. People often felt they had to cooperate in order to survive. Such profound powerlessness, combined with grief and loss, left many people depressed, passive, and easily controlled. "The result," Yvonne said, "is denial, self-loathing, and blocking out our own history. People only read about the negative impact of boarding schools and the statistics that reinforce an image of Native people as victims. What we're not doing is sharing 'good' information about Dakota people."

"For example, we could start our own school," Clifford said. "We could teach the language beginning at birth, Dakota thought, pictures, traditional ways of raising children. Develop our own societies and institutions rather than relying on wasichu institutions that perpetuate the unethical and immoral myth that Columbus discovered this country and that all American Indian tribes fought and killed each other. Native children are learning this in schools, reinforcing stereotypes and negative images. Instead, we need to teach about the seasonal cycles, about the importance of the spring and fall equinox, and the summer and winter solstice. We need to return to the cultural activities that were part of each season, from hunting to harvesting, storytelling in winter."

"The process of relearning how to raise beloved children starts," Gaby said, "with learning the fundamentals of family survival. You have to know what family you belong to as well as the stories and traditions of the tribe. If the family can survive, then the culture can survive, then the people can survive. In all cultures, the survival of the family is a priority. All of our stories tie you to your family, to your history."

"We owe loyalty to our families, remembering our kinship rules. You never bring shame upon your family. I didn't learn that lesson from Christianity," Clifford said.

There is a sense in this country that the mistakes of past generations are not the responsibility of those alive today. Yet in Germany, they've made each generation responsible for maintaining the history of what happened in the Holocaust. In the United States, we have yet to acknowledge that genocide has occurred within our own recent history, yet we spend billions to help restore foreign nations. "We ignore the insulting presence of an institution like Fort Snelling," Clifford said, "which should be given back to the Dakota people."

Gaby added, "We hear, 'you lost the war, so get over it.' If we can restore Kuwait, why can't we do that with American Indian people?"

Not only are we failing to teach a true understanding of the values and contributions of American Indian people in building this country, the underlying values that are being taught place us at great risk in not protecting our most valuable resources. "The Minnesota River is on the list of endangered rivers," Gaby pointed out. "To sustain life, we have to change direction. Our land and waters are endangered. This is a pivotal point in history. We want our institutions back. We want to have a good life for ourselves."

I learned a great deal in this first hour of conversation, but the real teaching came in what happened next.

As we continued to talk, not a single waitress approached our table, not even to bring water or to say that she was busy and would be right with us. Finally, Clifford called over one of the waitresses, a young Native woman who listened silently as Clifford calmly told her that we had been waiting for an hour and no one had come to take our order. She apologized, barely able to get the words out. He went on to tell her that the day before, he had to serve himself. She offered to take our order, but Clifford was not yet done. He said, "I want to speak to the manager." He also asked her to bring paper because he wanted to make a complaint.

The manager appeared and listened to Clifford restate his concerns. The manager said, "I'm sorry. We have two new waitresses, and they're just learning."

Clifford was not appeased. He was supported by Gaby and Yvonne, who confirmed his complaints. "If this was my restaurant," Clifford continued, drawing on his thirteen years managing a French restaurant in Chicago, "I would offer a free meal or at least a discount." Throughout this conversation, Clifford spoke in a voice that was firm but not abusive or angry. He was insistent on getting both acknowledgment and reparations for bad service. He wrote out a complaint on paper, dated it, and sent it around the table for all of us to sign.

It was this moment that would stay with me later, offering a model of assertive Native people rather than passive victims. Since then, I have thought back many times to this scene, replaying it in my own mind as I struggle with my own passive behavior. Even after Clifford complained, they still forgot my order, and yet I said nothing. I was focused on the interview, I rationalized, and not paying attention to the service. It was Yvonne who called the waitress back twice so that I finally had a sandwich to take home with me.

Until that afternoon, I had not given much thought to assertive behavior. I assumed that occasionally getting angry, maybe too angry, was the equivalent. What I learned was the difference in not allowing other people to disrespect you, whether it is intentional or through thoughtless behavior, even if it means challenging the dysfunctional behavior within your own family, your friends, and your community. Assertive is not the same as aggressive, nor does it come with anger. It simply means that I respect myself and so will you.

It seems easier at times to do or say nothing, only to have the repressed emotion surface later as excessive anger or binge drinking. To not slip into victim thinking when others patronize or insult you is a difficult challenge. You have to be present in a way that allows you to respond clearly and without rage. Otherwise, as Clifford would later explain, when you adopt the tactics of the bully, you become the bully.

In addressing difficult situations with these few simple steps of complaint, acknowledgment of harm, and reparations, we act in accordance with Dakota values, in a process that is similar to restorative justice. The key element at the restaurant was the assertiveness of the individuals in insisting on being treated with respect.

Later, when I asked Clifford what he considered to be one of the more encouraging changes today for Native people, he said it was "young people moving from being passive to being assertive." Similar, he added, to what happened in the restaurant. Native people live in a society that is patronizing, with an education system that portrays American Indians as invisible, forgotten, and inferior. The result is a tendency to become a passive victim, absorbing these attitudes as internalized racism.

Learning to be assertive is not easy, even for Clifford. When he was released from the army, he began to notice that when he drank, he became very angry, even aggressive. He asked himself why he was getting into fights and experiencing road rage when he was supposed to be having fun. His behavior while drinking showed him that he needed to come to a better balance in his life. He was stuffing all his anger by being a passive person in a society that was insulting him daily because he was Native. Clifford learned to "exercise my personal sovereignty in a positive way. Instead of being a passive victim, I became assertive."

Yet it's difficult to know when assertive behavior crosses a line into rage or self-righteous anger, and whether that too is sometimes necessary to draw attention to issues that have been ignored or buried for generations.

Sometimes in releasing the pent-up frustration and anger that is part of challenging long-term patterns of colonization, you can begin to do this work in a way that looks similar to those you are challenging. If you're being bullied and you respond in the same way, you are at risk of becoming a bully and losing your balance as a Dakota person. How do you resist injustice without becoming like the people who need to be challenged?

"You exercise personal sovereignty in a way that would be constructive, not destructive," Clifford said. "What I'm talking about is things like non-violent, peaceful actions. You can do things without being abusive. I think that takes early education. When you start at an early age, those things are imprinted in the mind so strong that it doesn't derail a person from doing the right thing for the right purpose. And also, walking with the spirits or walking with God or walking with Jesus and getting messages, called serendipity, outside ideas, outside concepts, outside input from the spirit world. This is very, very important." In other words, without the connection to the spiritual world, everything comes from the mind, creating an imbalance.

Changing attitudes and behavior takes time, conscious awareness, and a return to valuing yourself as a Dakota person. From a political perspective, this process is called "decolonizing," or freeing oneself from the mindset, beliefs, and values that reflect a dominant or colonizing culture. Often these beliefs have become so internalized that it is difficult even to see how our minds have been influenced. White cultural values are reinforced in every corner of our society, from the textbooks that are taught in schools to the way we grow food to the faces we see on television—none of them Native unless the story involves an arrest. For those of us whose families have come through boarding schools, who have lost the language, the ability to see our own colonized thinking requires years of unlearning.

At a gathering of Dakota people that was focused on the 1862 Dakota War and subsequent removal, Clifford asked the sixty people in the room how many had learned about this history growing up. Not a single person raised their hand. I had assumed that the people I met through the March had been raised within their culture, unlike the experience of my own family. And while many had lived on the reservation, the silence following Clifford's question was a stark reminder of how assimilation had affected every Native person in that room.

The process of decolonizing begins with the same observant presence that allows us to become assertive people. As a self-described "born-again Dakota," Clifford has survived the government's best attempts at assimilation and found his way back to his Dakota identity.

When Clifford got out of the service in 1960, the federal government was actively relocating Native people from reservations to big cities. After World War II, the heavy debt remaining from the war brought numerous challenges to ongoing federal support for Native tribes. This evolved into a policy of termination, or "liberating" Indians from the control of the BIA, breaking up reservations, abolishing tribal governments, and ending federal responsibility for the welfare of American Indian people. One aspect of termination was the 1952 Voluntary Relocation Program, which provided vocational training, moving expenses, and other support for Native families willing to move.

In 1940, approximately 8 percent of American Indians were living in urban areas. By the 2000 census, that number had increased to 64 percent. Between 1950 and 1980, an estimated 750,000 Native people migrated to the cities.

With his older brother already in the program, Clifford enrolled in culinary arts in Chicago, one of the original relocation cities. He became the chef/manager of a French restaurant, married, and raised five children. Finding his lifestyle to be fast-paced and stressful, Clifford was ready for a change when his mother called and said that his father had died and it was time to come home to the reservation. Not finding much work at home, he used his GI Bill to go back to school at the University of Minnesota, Morris.

"One day we bought a new house close to where I live now," Clifford said. "I bought a riding lawn mower, and I was cutting grass. Pretty soon all I heard was screeching cars, people fighting. No matter what I did, I couldn't change what was going on. I thought maybe if I went to divinity school, I could change their minds so that they could find a better way to live without all this anger and abuse and dysfunction happening. These were my relatives, so that made me go into the ministry." Two years later, he enrolled in divinity school at the University of Dubuque Theological Seminary. When the elders criticized him, he remembered his father's way of balancing Christianity with traditional beliefs.

Clifford's father, Elijah Canku, sang on the drum, hosted powwows on their land, and was also an elder in the Presbyterian Church. The elders criticized him for being a Christian and doing powwows, but he remained faithful to the church until he passed away from diabetes at age sixty-four. With many ceremonies outlawed while Clifford was growing up, Elijah was not able to provide him with a vision quest at age twelve. Instead, as Clifford was always "very spiritual minded," he joined the church. As he put it, both deal with God. From a young age, Clifford inherited his parents' ability to discern the spirit of God, whether as spirits that come while sharing his pipe or in receiving insight into Bible teachings.

After graduating from divinity school, Clifford found work as a teacher at Cook College and Theological School in Tempe, Arizona. He invited a group of young Dakota and Lakota men to practice on their drum at the school. This informal drum group used a tape recorder to copy the words for the songs they were learning. Clifford helped them translate the songs and understand the meaning, whether it was an honor song or a veteran's song. Playing on the drum, socializing at powwows, eating Indian food, and making friends all helped Clifford become a "born-again Indian singer." He tells people, "I was born again to my Indian identity. I just love being Dakota."

"But how," I asked, "do you reconcile your spirituality with Christianity, given what Christian churches have done to Native people?"

"There's no conflict," Clifford said. "When we were in seminary, all the students were given the opportunity to do directed study during summer to study any other kind of religion in the world. Me and another minister said, *Let's draw up a proposal so we can interview Indian people in Montana, South and North Dakota, and Nebraska.* We did interviews at different places. We had a survey: Are you participating in traditional spiritual ceremonies and ways of worship, and also are you Christian? Do you integrate them or keep them separate? After the summer was over, we started getting more into the vision quest, Sundance, participating in ceremony.

"I didn't see any conflict in the sense that the Bible is God's way of living, and the true traditions of the Dakota way of living are the Red Road. The two were very close. Both ways were walking with God. Where the conflict comes in is when you go outside the circle of true traditions. A lot of people were practicing false traditions, and they were betraying who they were. Some of them were saying, *I'm heyoka, I'm a clown,* but they were not because they were practicing false traditions, not the true traditions of being heyoka or clown within the circle. This one guy that we interviewed said, *yeah, I'm heyoka, I've been given permission to have seven wives.* We learned in our process that those are not traditions; those are dysfunctions. Also, in a Christian way, the same applies. There is a true practice of living Christian or misusing it for material gain. Or sexual gratification."

Has it been a struggle in the church world to combine what you do?

"When I went on a vision quest for the first time, one of the things that I caught, not audibly in words but as I was sitting there, I was asking for permission to practice in a traditional way. The thought came into my mind, a real conceptual thought saying, *This is real, my son; the traditional way of Dakota people is good.* That was the way for them to know who I am. *You can practice that because the blood of your ancestors is still in your body. You can practice that; you won't have no trouble.* The last thing I was told was that you can go the Christian way, too, same message.

"But the last thing he said was, *You can go the traditional way, but it's the people. You can go the Christian way; it's also the people.* I've pondered that question awhile. It's the people; what does that mean? Later on I figured out it's how you put it into practice, one way or the other. How do you use Christianity; how do you use the traditional way? The people can pervert it, or they can use it to better themselves. And really be happy." In other words, all those years of missionary work to convert the savages was not really Christian at all.

For Clifford, the question of balancing Native spirituality and Christian religion, which seems complex and contradictory on the surface, is simple and easily understood. Within the true teachings of any religion or spiritual practice are embedded values that instruct us how to live up to the highest potential of ourselves as human beings. At the core, they are all paths toward the creator, to the spirit, to God. "I always tell people, whatever makes you happy, walk in those ways," Clifford said.

But what if a person was not raised within their culture, as so many of us were not? Is it possible to relearn what was lost so that we can pass it on to our children and grandchildren? Clifford took my notebook and drew an image of a tree, describing the roots as a traditional Dakota person who was raised knowing his or her language and culture. A contemporary Dakota, which he said I was, was the upper part of the tree, someone who was poor in traditional experience but rich in experience with American institutions, a person who could have a house, career, and so forth, but who was not raised in traditional culture. The first step is to realize where you fit within this image. Do you know the language and traditions? Your family and their role in the social order? If not, then most likely you are beginning above ground, working to reestablish the roots of a Dakota cultural identity. "It's important," Clifford said, "to know where you are so that people know you're being truthful, you're honest, you're trying to learn the Dakota society."

Six months earlier, Clifford had sent me an e-mail about my memoir, *Spirit Car*, which he said was truthful, a comment that made me feel good. He also wrote that there was something missing in the book. Perhaps I already knew what that was, but he would be willing to talk with me about it.

When I finally had the chance to ask him, I was not afraid of what I might hear. *Spirit Car* was my first book as well as a first step in my own evolving identity as a Dakota woman. To receive guidance from Clifford was very important to the process of understanding Dakota culture. My intent in writing the book was to act as a witness to the impact of assimilation on my mother's family across five generations. It is part history, part personal memoir, and part story, because I wanted to take abstract words like *colonization* and render them with literary tools: show, don't tell the reader what that experience meant to real people.

Clifford hesitated only a moment before saying, "Your book lacks traditional thought," meaning it was not framed within the context of how Native people would traditionally view the world. I nodded my head. No argument there. In fact, the point of the book was that the first step in recovering cultural identity comes with knowing your own personal history as well as the larger history of what has happened in this country between whites and Native people. The book lacked traditional thought because I was not raised with that understanding but rather in schools that taught only white values and history. As a child growing up in a white suburb of Minneapolis, I was "imprinted" with the subtle Dakota lessons that came through my mother's way of parenting, the most significant part of our heritage that she carried forward. But we were not taught to understand the world from a traditional Dakota perspective.

Clifford's few words also helped me understand that I was there to interview him for precisely that reason: to gain a better understanding of traditional Native thinking. His critique was a gift, providing clarity and insight into the difficult process of recovering cultural knowledge.

At the core of this process is the concept of *WoDakota:* having the true traditions of the Dakota way of life. Every day is a learning experience, unraveling what you're supposed to do, becoming Dakota every day. As a teacher, Clifford is opening a doorway back to a traditional, disciplined way of life. "We have a mix of false traditions and true traditions," Clifford explained. "Iktomi [trickster] does not mean dysfunctional. True Iktomi spirit is you have to help the people. Some want to be hedonistic, follow false traditions."

Clifford stood near the window at the front of the classroom at Sisseton Wahpeton College, waiting as his students took their seats before learning the fundamentals of Dakota language. As always, Clifford was neatly dressed; his button-down shirt was carefully ironed, his jeans unwrinkled.

Behind large-frame glasses, his eyes observed the students, taking in their moods, the energy they brought into the room. Two young Dakota women came in pushing baby strollers that they parked next to their desks. A man closer to middle age took his place in the group. In this classroom, Dakota people of all ages are relearning how to speak their language.

I was reminded of a planning meeting a few years earlier that Clifford was leading in a college classroom. A woman came rushing in late, obviously hoping to slip in unnoticed. Clifford greeted her by name and thanked her for coming. Trained as she was to college rules enforced by shame and sarcasm, she began apologizing profusely. "No need to apologize," he said. "I'm just glad you're here." It was clear that he meant it.

Using a Beginning Dakota Language curriculum, which he cowrote with Nicolette Knudson and Jody Snow, Clifford instructed his students on correct pronunciation and word use. He wrote a simple sentence on the board: The dog is black. Then he wrote beneath it in Dakota: *Sunka kin he sapa.*

Clifford told his students to look at how the language works. We value "dog" more than "the," so *sunka* comes first in the sentence. While English is used as a common working language to communicate worldwide in business, science, and technology, Dakota is a highly descriptive, land-based language. For example, the word for cat is *ihmu,* meaning something that can expand its fur. The languages express very different worldviews, training the mind from its earliest days of communication.

"The Dakota always include children in their learning," Clifford said to the class. "It's good to have two babies here today."

Then Clifford asked his students to apply what they'd learned in a presentation. "Dakota people were very good cognitive people who could extract information and talk about it in real-life situations," Clifford said. "I'd rather have that than rote learning."

One of the consequences of boarding schools is the disruption in the traditional way of educating children. As generations of children grew up away from their families, they were not imprinted with these lessons, nor did they have role models for learning how to become parents. Many of the young men and women in Clifford's class were raised by parents who came through the boarding school system. They came to his class to learn their language, their history, and their culture.

One of Clifford's gifts as a teacher and as a spiritual leader is his ability to take conceptual ideas and beliefs and help people understand how to put them into practice in practical ways. Even if you've grown up completely separated from your language and culture, Clifford teaches college students how to read critically so that they can draw information on the process of becoming a Dakota man or woman from carefully chosen sources. A person who can understand and actualize these different stages will know how to initiate this process for a child. This is not meant to suggest that Dakota culture can be learned simply by reading a book. But for many individuals whose families no longer provide these teachings, this information, sometimes referred to as a "cognitive life raft," can offer the first steps on the road back to becoming a "born-again" Native.

Rather than using the term *parenting*, Clifford prefers to discuss the traditional ways of practicing the five stages of life. He uses Charles Eastman's *Indian Boyhood* and Ella Deloria's *Waterlily*, two books that capture many of the concepts and ceremonies that were part of a traditional way of life, especially with respect to gender roles. Clifford helps the students analyze the text to understand how parents were teaching their children the five stages of becoming a Dakota man or woman. Working slowly, students begin to see that at the very beginning of life, which is the first stage from infancy to two years old, children were taught how to use their five senses and to think conceptually beyond their own self-absorbed concerns.

For example, the cradleboard provided a straight back and support for a child's weak neck muscles. The child begins to use neck muscles to look around and become aware of the activity around him or her. As Charles Eastman explained, when children were stood up outside in a cradleboard, they learned to watch birds and squirrels and insects, becoming very aware of the natural world at an early age. "It really paid off for me," Clifford said. "I was very curious about life, curious about what goes on, very inquisitive." His first memory was of his grandfather bringing him beaded white moccasins when he was very young, giving him the sense of being cared for as a beloved child.

As the stages progress to boy/girl, ages three to ten; young man or woman, ages eleven to twenty; man/woman, ages twenty-one to forty-five; and older man or woman, ages forty-six to end of life, gender roles become firmly established within the expectations and institutions of the tribe. Dakota women were respected equals with Dakota men. Clifford teaches that Dakota women were "reared as young girls to be independent spirited, humble, and to raise their own children with remarkable patience, love, and kindness."

Embedded within the culture is a way of educating children throughout their lives to successfully achieve the challenges and lessons of each stage. Among the key concepts are *WoDakota,* the opportunity to improve character every day; Kinship Rules, learning early to respect and know your place within the family, household, extended family, and tribe; Birth Order, knowing your responsibility for functioning within the family; and the Five Stages, learning the educational steps taught in each stage of life.

"It's those kinds of things that I'm trying to instill in young men and women before they start having children," Clifford said. "Or even if they have children, they would say, *Oh, I need to get a cradleboard. I need to start to educate my child to be more conceptually oriented than me-me-me.*" Once students begin to see what they need to learn, they can find teachers who will help them improve every day. Providing for their own children what they did not receive in their own lives is another way of healing the past.

The other reason for teaching this information, Clifford said, is that "besides looking at the negative sides of boarding schools, we also need to share 'good' information about who we are." And part of that information is the Dakota model for practicing stages of life and the recognition that this model provides valuable lessons we all can still learn from today. In the novel *Waterlily,* Ella Deloria portrayed Dakota parents as loving, kind, and patient yet also very disciplined in the way they raised their children to become strong members of their community. Ceremonies like those for a "child-beloved" are poignant reminders of how deeply Dakota people have always cared for their children.

Now in the fifth stage of his own life, Clifford sees himself as an educator who wants to give back to the people what he was given. He feels a strong connection to Wacouta, a respected Dakota chief whose photograph he resembles and with whom he shares leadership qualities and character. With only thirteen fluent Dakota speakers left in Minnesota, the language is considered "unsafe" in terms of longevity. Clifford now teaches Dakota language, history, sociology, anthropology, and religious studies at North Dakota State University.

As he teaches Dakota language and culture, Clifford continues to search for an understanding of what his ancestors want him to do with his life. Working for justice in a peaceful way, remembering his ancestors with headstones and spirit plates, and serving as a go-between for this world and the spirit world are all ways in which Clifford works to understand his purpose.

"My calling is to be a spiritual leader," Clifford said. "You have to be true to what you're supposed to do. I just love it." He also recognizes that Dakota people are in different stages of healing, and he empathizes with those whose lives are stuck in trauma. In his own life, Clifford feels ready to move beyond the trauma to devote his energies to projects that tell other stories, from publishing the prisoners' letters to studying ancient medicine wheels and the work of Native science writers like Greg Cajete. Clifford is also committed to developing a new academic culture that encourages Dakota students to succeed. Thanks to his efforts, some of his students have now become teachers. "I'm honored by that," he said. "I feel so fulfilled that I've enabled them to get beyond feeling scared or not good enough. We have a lot to offer American society."

Yet Clifford's heart remains open to helping anyone who asks. The Dakota Letters Project, for example, has required a lot of dedication from Clifford over the past ten years of his life. "This is spiritual work," he explained. "A spirit came to me at the beginning. A call came the next day from Flandreau to start translating the letters. When you're selected by the spirit world, there's a reason. You feel obligated and privileged that they call on you. I feel a sense of duty to get this done. I would like the spirits to say, *You did what we wanted you to do; you were committed.* Then when I die, they say, *Come on home.* If someone asks you to do something, it's a great honor. If it takes a long time, that shows your Dakota values.

"Earning the approval of the spirit world," Clifford said, "is the most rewarding thing I could do in my life."

Gabrielle Tateyuskanskan

Gabrielle Tateyuskanskan

The horses were eager to be moving, stamping their feet as a cloud of warm breath rose above horse and rider. On this early December morning, just a few days before Christmas, about thirty riders were preparing to leave the Lower Sioux Reservation on a four-day ride along the Minnesota River to Mankato. They had begun several days earlier with a ceremony at the Crow Creek Reservation, and now the riders would continue following snow-covered country roads, absorbing the deep stillness of the frozen Minnesota River. Arvol Looking Horse, the keeper of the White Buffalo Calf Woman pipe, was riding with them for the last four days of this annual journey. As a chill wind moved through the eagle staffs at the front of the line, the Ride proceeded like an extended ceremony, bringing together prayer, healing relationships, and time spent in the breathtaking beauty of the Dakota homeland.

On the morning of December 26, weary horses would carry their riders into Reconciliation Park, where Dakota people and supporters gather each year to honor the thirty-eight men who were hanged in 1862. The Dakota 38 Memorial Ride was inspired by a recurring dream that came in 2005 to Jim Miller, a Lakota spiritual leader. Miller dreamed that he traveled 330 miles on horseback, arriving at a river in Mankato where he saw thirty-eight of his own ancestors hanged. As the staff carrier for the first four years of the ride, Miller retraced the route of his dream on horseback as a way of bringing healing and reconciliation. Through this event, Miller has given Dakota people a way to honor both this history and their long cultural relationship with horses and the Minnesota River Valley.

For the past four years, artist and poet Gabrielle Tateyuskanskan, an enrolled member of the Sisseton-Wahpeton Oyate on the Lake Traverse Reservation, has been part of this Ride with her partner, J. R. Rondell, also Sisseton-Wahpeton Oyate; Gaby's two children, Vivienne and Hunter; and her mother, Yvonne Wynde. They ride their own horses, transporting them from their land at the Old Agency to the Lower Sioux Reservation. For Gaby, who grew up traveling the roads along the Minnesota River Valley with her grandmother, the Ride means returning to a landscape she loves and sharing a deeply spiritual event with her family.

The Ride also allows Gaby to spend time with their horses, a relationship that has both inspired and supported her throughout her life. Gaby said, "Horses are sacred animals that have sustained the people through these tough periods. Riding horses in this beautiful scenery in the winter strengthens something in my spirit." Dakota people have long relied on horses for hunting, moving camp, and warfare. In the late eighteenth century, horses were rounded up and slaughtered by the government as a way of preventing Native people from leaving their reservations. Events like the Dakota 38 Ride help reestablish the strong relationship between Dakota people and horses, whom they called *s'unkawakan,* or sacred dog, based in mutual dependence and affection.

While Gaby credits both her grandmother and her mother for helping her become an artist, the early days she spent as a child helping her grandmother garden developed her imagination. At the Old Agency in Sisseton, Gaby's grandmother Vivian Barse Wynde rose early each morning as the birds were just beginning to sing, preferring to work while the sun was still cool. She made cowboy coffee in a chipped enamel pot that sat on a grill over her cooking fire, ready for friends who stopped by to visit and tell stories. Gaby and her cousins learned how to plant seeds that had been saved from the previous harvest, how to weed, when to pick the ripe vegetables. Seeds were saved for no more than two years. Vivian grew sweet corn for drying and kept a separate garden on her land at Enemy

Swim, where she could raise hominy corn without worrying about cross-pollination. She also showed her grandchildren how to plant a traditional Three Sisters garden.

"She would say, *Get a mound of earth, plant six corn kernels in the middle, then plant whatever beans you wanted around the outside, and the squash in the middle sections*," Gaby said. "Then she would talk about how she was raised by her grandmother and her great-grandmother. Her mother died from tuberculosis when she was a baby. She was taught by women who were the generation that left Minnesota. Dakota was her first language."

Gaby's grandmother was also a storyteller, a woman who was generous in sharing what she knew with her grandchildren. "She would tell both historical stories and the Creation stories, the older Dakota stories, stories about what supposedly happened at certain places," Gaby said. "That's why I got an interest in history."

When the other kids grew bored and threw clods of dirt at each other or wandered away to play with friends, Gaby stayed close to her grandmother's side. From a young age, she was interested in all that her grandmother was teaching, especially her stories and the way they sparked her imagination. She knew that when it was just the two of them pulling weeds together or picking chokecherries, Gaby could ask her grandmother all of the questions that raced through her active mind. They formed a close bond, each one relying on the other.

When she grew older, Gaby began to travel with her grandmother as she visited friends and relatives in Minneapolis and at various reservations. Refusing to listen to the car radio, Vivian told stories as a hot wind blew through the open windows, weaving her voice through the daydreams of the drowsy child in the seat next to her. In hunting season, Vivian would take Gaby with her to picnic at Enemy Swim so she could check that hunters weren't trespassing on her land. She would do the same thing at Crow Creek, making sure the farmer wasn't overgrazing her pasture.

Vivian always stopped at historic sites along the way. Many of her trips were between Sisseton and Minneapolis, where Gaby was born in 1955 and where they still had relatives. They followed the Minnesota River Valley with stops at Birch Coulee, where she told Gaby about the battle that took place there during the 1862 Dakota War.

Depending on the season, sometimes they spent time in the woods gathering wild foods and medicines like mint, chokecherries, wild plums. She taught Gaby about the medicinal plants that are easy to recognize and use, plants that have antiseptic properties or soothe bug bites. Gaby learned which plants needed their roots protected so they would grow back and which needed enough flowers left on them so the seeds would reestablish new plants.

"When she taught me about the plants that have heavy medicinal uses, it was about the importance of valuing those things and being the kind of person who could protect them so they're not abused," Gaby said. Then her grandmother would tell long stories about her own grandmother, how she was taught to put down tobacco and to respect life.

Unlike the elders who maintain their silence about the past, Gaby's grandmother did her best to answer Gaby's questions. She told Gaby about her time at the Tipi Zi School, how she was punished for speaking her language. Her grandparents, hearing that she was mistreated, kidnapped her from the school, hiding out on an isolated piece of land until the authorities stopped searching for her.

"But why?" Gaby asked, already a child whose depth of understanding far exceeded her years. "Why would your grandparents send you to a school when people knew that they were mistreating kids?"

There was a pause, a moment of silence while Vivian looked off into the distance, seeing something that held her motionless for just an instant before she answered. Her voice never changed, nor her willingness to tell Gaby what she knew, but something in her body shifted, a weight pressed on her shoulders. She said that people felt so powerless after the chiefs were killed that they felt they had to do what the government wanted. But it was there in her eyes, a deep sorrow that remained even as she turned back to the garden.

When they were done gardening for the day, sometimes Gaby would lie on her back in the long grass looking at different clouds as they moved across the broad prairie sky, imagining horses in the various shapes. Her favorite Creation story was about a black stallion that lived in the thunder-clouds. She could see the horse in the sky above her, wispy clouds forming his mane and tail, his hooves flashing lightning. She named him Cumulo-Nimbus after a cloud she had just learned about in school. "I think I really identified with the spirit of the horse," Gaby explained.

The images she carried in her mind began to spill out onto paper, on the walls of her bedroom, taking shape in colors and lines and paint. She had a large roll of white paper that she unrolled on the front yard, bending over her watercolor painting as her unruly hair pulled free from her braids, teased by a prairie wind that also dried her paints. She used charcoal from the fire to draw, mixed paint with pencils, added crayons to her images. Her mother and grandmother encouraged her, appreciated her work, left the drawings untouched on the walls of her room.

From her grandmother, Gaby learned that "everybody should have self-respect. Their identities, whoever they are, should be respected." When a teacher said something inappropriate about Indians or mistreated Gaby, her grandmother marched into school and confronted the teachers and the principal. Sometimes she brought Gaby's mother, Yvonne, also a fearless advocate for her children. But as the family matriarch, Vivian was ferocious in her protection of her grandchildren. "That was my experience being the beloved child," Gaby said. "I don't think it was meant for racist teachers, but it saved me."

As Gaby would learn throughout her years in public schools, her unwillingness to tolerate mistreatment would also make her life more difficult at a time when she was too young to defend herself. In the third grade, she showed her mother an essay she had written about Christopher Columbus, stating that he did not discover America because Native people were already here. Her mother, an educator, was very proud. She asked, "What did your teacher say?"

"I didn't hand it in," Gaby replied, "because I knew it wasn't what she wanted."

Even at that young age, Gaby understood all too well the consequences of challenging people in authority who were not ready for the truth. She talked back to her teachers, became argumentative, spent a lot of time in the principal's office waiting for her mother or grandmother to pick her up. She was soon marked as someone who would "come to no good in life." By high school, she was in a rage at how she was treated in school. After growing up with women who had taught her that her identity was important, the people who were supposed to give her a formal education seemed more focused on taking that identity away. "I grew up believing that there should be justice. I knew I was going to disappear in anger and never develop my talents," Gaby said. "I knew I wouldn't make it at a reservation school."

Instead, she took the bold, if seemingly ironic, step of attending a Native-run boarding school in New Mexico. Boarding schools had evolved over time. In 1928, nearly fifty years after the first boarding school was established, the Brookings Institution released the Meriam Report, which severely criticized the administration, living conditions, and curriculum used in these schools. Conditions improved somewhat so that during the Depression, destitute families relied on boarding schools to help support their children. My mother's family enrolled her and four older sisters whenever there was no work available and her parents were unable to feed their nine children. Improvements were gradual and uneven, with continuing reports of abuse, but during the next several decades, tribes began to assume control of schools that were previously run by the federal government or churches.

With her strong talent for art, Gaby chose the newly formed high school at the Institute of American Indian Arts (IAIA) in New Mexico. She was mentored by Otelli—the wife of a famous Hopi jeweler, Charles Lolana—who encouraged her to take her art seriously. Otelli also told Gaby, "I can tell by your behavior that you've been raised really well. You must come from a really nice family."

During her junior and senior high school years, Gaby attended IAIA, where she worked with well-known Native artists, writers, and filmmakers, including T. C. Cannon, R. C. Gorman, Kevin Red Star, and Simon Ortiz. While she was still angry and frustrated that schools like this did not exist in South Dakota, she was surrounded by artists who were struggling with similar issues around identity, creativity, and defining Native art. Not only was she developing her technical skills in a wide variety of disciplines; she had people to talk with who understood the challenge of developing an individual voice as an artist, especially as a Native artist.

"I was trying to figure out, how do I learn about who I am?" Gaby said. "How do I communicate that through my artwork in a way that's really my own? I like doing beadwork and making my traditional outfits. How do I really express who I am through this? How am I going to do that without it being stereotyped? I really struggled with that."

Coming from the Northern Plains, Gaby knew instinctively that to develop her own voice, she would need to understand fully who she was and what ideas were important for her to communicate. Even now at fifty-five, Gaby said, "I'm still figuring it out. I know that I'm really tied to the land, to the landscape where I'm from. It's shaped and healed me."

Gaby attended college at IAIA for one year before deciding that she needed to learn more about Native history and social justice issues. The same restless search that first brought her to IAIA kept her moving to Fort Lewis College in Durango, Colorado, where they had an Indian studies program. She could not yet define exactly what it was she was searching for, but she was drawn to psychology, sociology, and Indian studies, reading the work of indigenous writers throughout the hemisphere. As a visual artist, she had never considered becoming a writer, but studying with Paula Gunn Allen convinced her that she needed a narrative to explore the questions she was grappling with. Long before the term *historical trauma* was even conceived, Gaby was already struggling to understand how Native people heal from their genocidal history and the oppression that continues to this day. Throughout her life, this search for understanding would become an essential part of Gaby's work to define her artistic voice.

After graduation, she continued her study of art in Boston at the School of the Museum of Fine Arts, focusing on drawing and painting. She was fascinated by the philosophy of art—in particular, taking courses to understand what defines Native art. In traditional Native cultures, there was no word that defined art as separate from daily life.

For a young Dakota artist, however, this difference also raises many questions. Is art something that society pushes artists to create because they like the old culture, preferring romanticized images to the reality of contemporary Natives, or is it a form of self-expression? She was searching for a way to convey her passion for her work, a process so intense that sometimes she could even taste the colors of her paints and beads.

When her beloved grandmother passed away, Gaby returned to Minneapolis and finished her degree in art education at the College of St. Catherine. When she was ready to teach, she moved back to Sisseton. Not surprisingly, the same school system she couldn't survive in as a child was no easier for her to navigate as an adult.

While struggling to find work, she continued to dance at powwows, both jingle and traditional. One of her friends, J. R. Rondell, a traditional dancer, eventually became her partner. Together they raised Gaby's two children, whose father had passed on when they were still young. Her older son, Sage, was already in college. Gaby continued to develop her artwork, placing it in collections at the Heritage Center of Red Cloud Indian School, the South Dakota Cultural Heritage Center in Pierre, St. Joseph's Indian School, and the Woodrow Wilson Keeble Memorial Health Care Center. She found part-time work teaching painting and drawing at Sisseton Wahpeton College, a job that left time for her family, her creative work, and her increasing involvement in activist issues.

I waited for Gaby at the Crossroads Restaurant at the Dakota Connection Casino in Sisseton, South Dakota, the same restaurant where I met her with Clifford for lunch a year earlier. Today, to my relief, the service was perfect. Confrontation is still not my best skill, especially after five hours of driving. The last one hundred miles on Highway 28, a two-lane blacktop road that runs a straight line from Sauk Centre to Sisseton, was a white-knuckle experience. A light snow whipped across the open prairie, hiding the lines of the road, piling up in sudden drifts, and compacting into a layer of ice along my side of the lane.

Yet there were moments of exquisite beauty as well. When I could relax enough to look across the prairie, I saw gray-white clouds and unbroken fields of snow form a seamless landscape that was blurred by a haze of tiny snowflakes. The peeling paint on an old white shed revealed the same gray-brown tone of dry wood as the windbreak of trees along the horizon. This was a harsh landscape, frightening in its isolation, breathtaking in its subtlety. A land where life cannot be taken for granted.

When Gaby walked in to the café, she moved swiftly across the room, her easy stride evidence of her early years as an athlete in school, riding horses, gardening, spending long hours outdoors. Her dark hair waved in abundant curls around a youthful face. It's easy to see why a man once told her mother, "When your daughter gets married, somebody is going to give you a lot of ponies for her."

I tell her about my white-knuckle drive and she laughs, nodding her head in sympathy. People who grow up on the Lake Traverse Reservation learn early about the extremes of South Dakota seasons: the prairie winds that bury roads in winter return in summer as hot, dry gusts that swirl dust devils across the fields.

"My grandmother really taught me to appreciate earth," she said. The South Dakota landscape has also inspired her as an artist and provided solace in its unique beauty. Where another person might see only desolation in this landscape, Gaby observes it with an artist's eye. "Even watching snow drift across the plains like sand in subzero killer weather is beautiful and part of the imagery that I like," Gaby said.

The years she spent with her grandmother in the garden, gathering plants in the woods, and lying on her back watching horses take shape in the clouds taught Gaby that nature can heal, providing a place where she can let go of her anger and pain. In her watercolors, she often paints landscapes and images of Native people dancing, sharing her understanding of the prairie wind by showing how it moves through the fringe and feathers on traditional outfits. "I'm no longer searching for exactly how I belong to all this," Gaby said. "It's in my spirit. Woven into the fabric of who you are, are all these things that make your identity really solid when you get to be an adult."

I had first met Gaby at the 2002 Dakota Commemorative March, which she cofounded with Leo Omani and Waziyatawin Angela Wilson. I knew her to be an eloquent speaker whose words came from her heart, while she often allowed others to assume more visible leadership roles. During one of the Marches, I overheard an elder refer to her as "gifted," meaning that she has spiritual gifts, just as Phyllis Roberts, the elder who carries the canupa, and Clifford Canku are gifted. Her innate sensitivity as an artist, poet, and deeply intuitive being has often helped provide guidance for the March. Even her name, Tateyuskanskan, which means "wind spirit" or "something that moves but you can't see it," is a fitting description of the work that Gaby does quietly, often behind the scenes, wary of the distractions of public leadership. She is a fearless yet compassionate protector of the spiritual intent that she sees as the purpose of the commemorative walk.

At the 2010 March, I was standing behind one of the vans that carry the sacred items Phyllis brings with her, a vehicle that follows the canupa. A white couple had come for the first time and brought their small dog with them. Since they did not have a car and we would be walking about twenty miles that day, they put their dog in the van with the sacred items. Gaby appeared almost immediately as they were getting the dog settled. Speaking in a straightforward, calm tone, she told the couple that they were essentially offering their dog as a ceremonial sacrifice by putting him in that van. They immediately grabbed him, a look of stunned surprise on both faces, as they began to apologize. Gaby smiled, accepted their apologies, and then returned to her place at the front, where she assists Phyllis in carrying the canupa.

Oglala Lakota artist Arthur Amiotte, whose work is inspired by his love of Lakota traditions and ceremonies, explained once to Gaby that he was a ceremonialist. He said, *I'm not the spiritual leader. I'm someone who helps make the ceremony work.* His words, and the way he combines his spirituality with his artwork, made a strong impression on Gaby. He helped her define a role that fit with her deeply held beliefs, a role that is expressed in the mindful way she participates in events like the commemorative walk.

One of those ways is to be sensitive to the exquisite moments that are also part of this event. Sometimes during the early days of the March, we walked along the river on dirt roads nearly empty of traffic. As the sun melted the frost on the long grass and our breath rose like plumes on the cold morning air, we walked past deep woods with the river at our side. One morning, we slowly approached a large fenced field on our left where four horses stood grazing. As we drew closer, their heads raised, and they watched our slow-moving procession; they listened to the drum in the powwow music we played. The horses began to walk together at a measured pace, as if the rhythm of our steps inspired them to join us in their own way. They trotted down the field, shoulder to shoulder, and then turned as a group, moving through a large loop, all the while remaining together as if choreographed. They danced up and down the field, turning and wheeling, heads high, their bodies saying, *We witness your grief, your long walk, your courage; we send you the strength of our own steps.* We could all see that something astonishing was happening. These horses were dancing for us, and with us.

Beneath the beauty that we witnessed, the grief that we shared, and the attention that was given to healing during this long walk, there was another aspect, a call to arms, an insistence that we also raise our voices in protest against the harms done to Dakota people. This dichotomy of politics intertwined with the spiritual produced two powerful publications featuring Dakota voices: a special edition of *American Indian Quarterly* and *In the Footsteps of Our Ancestors: The Dakota Commemorative Marches of the 21st Century*. The latter, edited by Waziyatawin Angela Wilson, is a stunning collection of photographs, essays, poetry, and stories.

Yet there is also an inherent tension in this dichotomy, in the innate differences between two approaches to healing for Dakota people. After years of observing Gaby's skill in providing spiritual direction when needed, her humility as a leader, and her willingness to confront injustice directly, I had come to Sisseton to ask her how she balanced political activism with the spiritual process of healing from historical trauma. I was also interested in her work as an artist, her thoughts on forgiveness, and the challenges she has faced in raising her own beloved children.

↩

In Gaby's family, there is a long history of speaking out against injustice, providing role models that inspire each generation. "In our family, we have the tradition that the children are beloved to the point that you have to do acts of resistance," Gaby said. Her grandmother and her mother were both kidnapped by family from boarding schools and then hidden until they were safe. Her mother, Yvonne Wynde, went on to become a vice president at Oglala Lakota College on the Pine Ridge Reservation and a lifelong educator.

Yvonne's father was descended from David Eastman, the older brother of Charles Eastman, a well-known doctor, philosopher, and author of *Indian Boyhood*. As scholar David Martínez wrote in *Dakota Philosopher: Charles Eastman and American Indian Thought,* Eastman was a true philosopher because of "his capacity to see through to the essence of things, whether it is being a Dakota or a Christian or the nature of modern life."

Despite attending medical school and studying Christianity, Eastman never lost his sense of himself as a Dakota man. As a small boy, he was exiled with his family after the 1862 Dakota War. He served as the physician for the wounded after the massacre at Wounded Knee. Throughout his life, he was deeply interested in matters dealing with Native rights and published nine books as well as shorter works.

Gaby's mother used to take her and her siblings to the old bookstores in Minneapolis, searching for first editions of Charles Eastman's work. Gaby grew up reading his books, training her mind and developing an interest in philosophy. She may not have completely understood them at the time, but she knew even then that they were important to the family.

In one of Gaby's photos, Charles's sister, Mary, is wearing braids, round glasses, and a fur coat as she stands next to him. Their mother, the granddaughter of the Santee chief Cloud Man, married Jacob Many Lightnings, a warrior who fought with Inkpaduta. Mary Eastman married a mixed-blood, David Faribault, and was imprisoned at Fort Snelling and removed to Crow Creek. David Faribault was a fluent speaker of both English and Dakota and wrote many of the letters now preserved in the Dakota Letters Project.

"I learned from them a great respect for life because there's been so much tragic loss," Gaby said. Her grandmother used to tell how her great-grandmother's father disappeared in the 1862 Dakota War and the family never learned what happened to him. When she offered her spirit plate, her prayers were full of sadness. After hearing that story, Gaby said that spirit plates became much more meaningful to her as a ritual. Like many of the generation whose relatives disappeared, Mary Eastman was always concerned that her relatives had headstones marking their graves.

Gaby learned at a young age that "your family, the landscape, who you are as a tribal person, are all valuable and worth protecting. It's bigger than you. I learned that leadership is not about charisma. It's about people who really care for other people." When Gaby was living in Pine Ridge in 1973 at the time of the Wounded Knee occupation, she had an opportunity to see firsthand the consequences of violent activism. Describing it as a war zone, she remembered her mother telling her not to do beadwork by the window because she might get shot. People she knew were getting killed while urban Natives who had come to join AIM would simply disappear.

"That's where I got the impression that violence was not a good way to change anything," Gaby said. She also knew the children of some of the AIM leaders who weren't being taken care of by their parents. She saw the price they paid for their parents' activism: "That's why for me, my family is really important in doing activist things, because I saw what happens if you spend too much time on activism and abandon your family."

She also learned the dangers of charismatic leadership, seeing how easy it is to become pulled into a myth created by the media. As Severt Young Bear wrote, being a leader can make you greedy for power and willing to do foolish things if you let it, to the point of neglecting your own family. Instead, for chiefs who used to be lifetime leaders, "there's no room for greed or jealousy or petty personal things. If you're going to be that leader, you have to watch yourself and maintain self control." To be an effective leader today, "you would have to be able to be a silent eater and slow thinker, to be serene and give advice and encouragement, to give half of your body to your group or your people, to have a very understanding [wife] and family who are behind you and support you."

When her friends took off from art school to join the occupation of the BIA building in Washington, DC, Gaby turned down the invitation to join them. Although she was deeply interested in what they were doing, she never felt drawn to be part of getting arrested at protests. Instead, her activism emerged from daily acts of self-defense on behalf of herself and her family. Like the time she drove to Walmart to buy decorations for a birthday party for her young nieces, who were between the ages of two and four.

"I was thinking, how am I going to take all these little kids to Walmart? The easiest way would be to put them all in a shopping cart and just whiz over to the balloon and crepe paper section. I had visions of herding crickets once we got in there. I put them in the cart, and we were trying to whiz through the store without losing somebody. This woman comes up to me and says, *Haven't you ever heard of birth control?* I wanted to lay into her, but I thought, if I stop this cart, these kids are going to jump out. I just said, *Beat it, lady, before I call security.*" When you have to defend yourself against people like that in the world, then there's little appeal in getting arrested, as much as Gaby values the efforts of those who are willing to do this work.

Or, as Denise Breton suggests in *The Mystic Heart of Justice,* consider Plato's edict that *each of us do what is ours to do.* Justice is best served when we know who we are. As Breton says, "By using our time, energies, and resources to do what's ours, we do justice to ourselves by fulfilling our mission, and we do justice to our communities and world by contributing what they most need that we have to offer."

For Gaby, raising children on the reservation has meant facing many of the same challenges that she knew as a child. "It's still a punitive school system. It's still a society that doesn't want to admit that in order for democracy to exist in America, they sacrificed indigenous people." Gaby's children, and those of every Native family, bear the weight of what it means to be indigenous in a country that wants to let that harsh history fade away. Not only are children inheriting an intergenerational legacy of pain and sorrow, they still face prejudice and discrimination in their daily lives.

"How do you show your children that they're beloved to you when the minute they're born, you might as well say *you have to be a mini-warrior*?" Gaby said. "That's really hard, especially when there are other issues going on with families.

"I think that's one of the reasons why there's such a high suicide rate among young people," Gaby explained. "They're so young, and yet they have to navigate this difficult burden." They're expected to educate teachers and people in mainstream society on the issues when they're just beginning to learn about it themselves. They're expected to forgive people for what they've done to their ancestors and to their tribes. "That's just way too much for kids when they're trying to figure out their own identity and what it means to be a tribal person." Especially when this history is still not taught in school.

When Gaby's oldest son, Sage, was studying Christopher Columbus in school, he came home one day really mad. He said, "You know, when I tried to bring up the point that there were Indian people here, the teacher didn't want to listen."

Gaby asked him, "So what did you do about it?"

He said, "I told my friends, *never mind what she says. I'll tell you the truth at recess.*" While Gaby laughed as she told this story, it was heartbreakingly evident how little has changed for her children.

Fortunately for her family, Gaby said, they had many generations who knew how important it was to speak up. From her own experience feeling the protection of her grandmother, mother, and great aunt, Gaby has worked to extend this same model of protection to her children. Her son Hunter at twelve was beaten by a bully at school with a jump rope that left welts across his back, arms, and even his hands as he tried to defend himself. She went to school and demanded an explanation. She asked, "If he had come from my house looking like this, what would you have done?"

"We would have called social services or child protection," was the reply.

Gaby said, "Guess what? You didn't tell me this happened, and he came home from school looking like this. I'm reporting you." She contacted social services, informed the sheriff, and hired an attorney. Despite her efforts, no one was able to explain where the teachers were while this was happening at recess. Nor did anyone ever apologize, telling her that it was a case of boys will be boys. Finally, with little help from the attorney, she persuaded the South Dakota Department of Education to sanction his school. They were given ten days to improve their systems.

"When I saw those whip marks on Hunter, it just broke my heart," Gaby said. "It was all I could do not to cry. I knew if I started crying, Hunter would never heal. You're in shock, but another part of you has to take over and be matter of fact: *Okay, we're going to the doctor; we're getting an attorney.* I needed my mother and sister to make sure that I didn't leave out anything, make sure that I didn't burst into tears when I needed to be talking and convincing. That stuff takes a toll on you. I had other outlets like dancing, which is a physical thing. You can put your emotions into something and do it really hard, and it's appropriate. You can release some of that. Go to a sacred site and connect with that place and what it's about. What you don't have the answers to, put it in the hands of the Creator. If I didn't have those tools, I don't know if I would have been able to fight for my children like I did."

She took Hunter to see a child psychologist, but he refused to talk. She tried taking him to ceremony and also to see Clifford Canku. Worried that he might have trouble developing relationships after this incident, she decided that he needed a champion, a living being that he could trust. So she bought him a horse. They kept the horse in the backyard, where it wandered around like a big dog. In the summer, he would sleep by Hunter's window and press his head to the screen. A friend said that Hunter and his horse exemplified the saying about a horse and rider becoming one being. Hunter continues to ride his horse during the Dakota 38 Ride. He went on to become one of the 39 percent of Native males who graduate high school in South Dakota.

Their daughter, Vivienne, is an exceptionally bright young woman who suffered from the low expectations set for Native students by teachers who assumed that she couldn't do the work. After she received little encouragement from counselors, Gaby persuaded Vivienne to apply to Ivy League colleges. She was awarded a full scholarship to Wellesley College, where she is studying environmental science. Gaby continues to teach her about ancestral environmental knowledge, providing a cultural context for the modern lessons that Vivienne is learning at school.

Looking back, Vivienne can see how a lot of what the teachers and staff did at her border town public school was wrong. She also commented to her mother that she didn't realize what a big deal it was to have opportunities to participate in cultural life. Vivienne had her Womanhood ceremony, and she and Hunter both participated in ceremonial life and dance. Vivienne had taken it for granted that that's what everybody's parents did.

Gaby stressed to both of her children that they had great potential. She used to read Creation stories to them about Star Boy, who was the champion for those who experienced injustice. She wanted them to learn that bad things happen in the world, but it's no reflection on who you are. "There is a long history of oppression for the Dakota Oyate," Gaby explained, "and you have to find your way through it. But when you get tired, the family is there ready to help. You're not alone." In moments of despair, when it seemed there was too much stacked against them, Gaby was there to say, "No, you can do this. I believe in you."

Of all that has been lost from traditional child-raising practices due to generations raised in boarding schools, the loss of someone to believe in your potential as a child, who is willing to protect and stand up for you, has deeply harmed Native children. Without that parent or grandparent or champion, many of these children simply fall through the cracks. Young girls become sexually active and have children while they're still children themselves. Young men find their masculinity assaulted on a daily basis as they're told they will never get a job, never graduate. As children, they are powerless to fight against authority.

Even with a supportive family, it takes years to figure out all the issues and baggage that result from assaults on identity. For Gaby, her creative work has provided a way for her to "communicate that harsh, brutal voice about the experience of the past. The rage and sorrow that's really deep, to the point that a lot of people don't even survive. I knew that's what I had to figure out, or I wasn't going to survive. If you can't validate what you're feeling and thinking and you get isolated, you don't survive. When you have children, then you have to help them with that."

Through their artwork, artists like Gaby can provide contemporary society another way of seeing and understanding who we are, challenging the Hollywood stereotypes that are barriers to perceiving the richness of Dakota culture. For example, despite the hardships that Dakota people have experienced, the artistry and craftsmanship of flute players and beadwork demonstrate the sophistication with which Dakota people wove beauty into daily life. "The tragedy of the war has to be told," Gaby said. "But these other connections are also part of the full story. They're what help us heal from the trauma."

Art can also open a window into perspectives that non-Natives may not fully understand. Difficult history, such as the forced removal of Dakota people from Minnesota, can be rendered into story, film, and paintings that communicate a sense of loss, how it feels to be exiled from your homeland. We all know what it means to feel loss, especially those who have lost a home through fire or eviction or who have experienced homelessness. Artists help us see and absorb these deep connections between human experiences, creating a bridge for understanding.

"If you look at a harsh issue from a safe place, you can begin to have an understanding," Gaby explained. "People are sensitive and want to do the right thing. If you approach them in a nonthreatening way, that helps create social change. As artists, we want to get these stories out to a diverse audience so we can make these connections. It's the same with spiritual work. We're sharing ways that make us better human beings. Whether you learn this in solitude with the landscape or wherever you get your spiritual connection, it helps you become sensitive to ethics and morality."

Gaby's artwork has also helped her find ways to communicate the duality of her experience, how a landscape that was the site of a battle can also hold memories of a picnic with her grandmother. She has learned to accept both aspects of life, understanding that the harsh experiences teach you resilience and strength, while the happy times sustain you and give you hope.

"I'm really grateful for that gift of appreciating the landscape and seeing the spirit in nature and understanding how healing that is," Gaby said. "Being able to put my anger someplace. Letting it go, putting it in the Creator's hands and going on to do other things."

From Gaby's appreciation of the natural world grew a desire to protect the sacred sites left by the ancestors. "Besides the beloved child, there was also the love for the unborn," Gaby said. "Our ancestors would leave things so their relatives could have things when they came. That's why we have all these sacred sites; they knew we were coming. They sang us into existence." By spending time at these places, we can begin to understand why our ancestors chose them and what they can teach us about the world.

"Even if you don't know how to do the rituals that are attached to some of the places, you can enrich your life just by understanding that history and what the sites were used for," Gaby explained. "Our ancestors used the natural environment to heal their inner spirits. That's a significant thing to discover about human sensitivity."

Simply walking on the land, on the long Coteau des Prairies that was left between two streams of glacial ice, feeling the wind on your skin, listening to the call of a red-tailed hawk can remind you that the ancestors walked this same land, leaving things behind for those to come. On her walks in early spring or late fall when the grasses are thin, Gaby has found old rock formations shaped like lizards and turtles, cairns, vision quest sites, and even pictographs.

A few years earlier, Gaby worked with the Tribal Historic Preservation Office (THPO) to map various sites so that they could be protected from vandals and collectors. If you've lost your connection with the ancestors, with the sense of this land as a sacred "Dakota cathedral," then it's easy to rationalize taking artifacts that seem to be placed in the middle of nowhere, such as the thunderbird rocks—rocks that bore the claw marks of the great battle fought between two thunderbirds—that disappeared.

"Being alone in nature gives us an emotional connection that we need," Gaby said. "When I'm walking on the prairie, I wonder what the ancestors were thinking. Why they left things. As an artist, it's aesthetically pleasing to see how wide the world is, the eastern horizon, even a glimmer of Lake Traverse. These things are bigger than humans. It feels hopeful to think about this ancient knowledge, how life will go on.

"I have a strong sense of people caring for me before I was even here. It's understanding that all your relatives, everybody in the community who come to know you, will do their part to protect you and make sure you grow up to be a fine human being. So that you realize and play this important role that you're meant to have in life." Protecting the sacred essence of who we are, the unique voice we each carry, and the understanding that we are all beloved children is part of what has lain dormant for generations who have been assaulted by assimilation programs.

"I think sometimes it lay dormant because some things were just too full of sorrow in those generations to be able to tell you about it," Gaby explained. "It was such an unbearable sorrow. It wasn't because they didn't want you to know. When you're so emotional and hurt, your throat just tightens up and you can't speak."

But finding ways to speak is essential to protect what we love from harm. Gaby is among those who can be counted on to write letters and voice her opinion at public forums on issues that threaten Dakota land and people. When the Big Stone coal plant was spewing mercury into the lake system, when they used water from the tribe's aquifer while poor tribal members had to purchase water from the Missouri River, she spoke up. "We want to protect our old culture, but we can't because of what modern society is doing," Gaby said.

When her family was mistreated by teachers and the educational system, they responded by becoming teachers and educators. This is a profound way to address harm; by changing the system that has harmed you and your family, you are indeed healing yourself, your ancestors, and future generations.

Equally important, however, is the compassion that tempers Gaby's willingness to confront injustice. "My grandmother taught me to respect life," she explained. "When you have that understanding, then you're real careful how you treat others. I think our ancestors knew that. That's why there were ceremonies for our warriors to come back into camp. They knew that being involved in violence paid a hard price on your psyche."

She told a story from a book she was reading, *Unbroken,* about a man who survived brutality in a Japanese prisoner-of-war camp. He was struggling to understand how human beings can get caught up in being brutal and in justifying it. At the end of the book, the protagonist goes back and finally meets the Japanese officer who was so brutal to him. He asked him, "Why did you do those things to me?"

He replied, "I thought I was being a good soldier."

"Part of our history was so hurtful that if you're a perpetrator, it's easy to let it fade in memory," Gaby said. "If you're part of the hurt, you want the hurt to stop, so it's easy to let it fade into memory. Because it's such a powerful story, it keeps pushing back until you deal with it. If we're going to stop people from brutalizing each other, we can't forget that this happened. When you get the mob mentality and you're not thinking anymore, you do some really brutal things. All of a sudden, that situation is not there anymore. What does that do to people who are part of doing brutal things? I think the difficulty is to have people admit that their families were part of brutality like that. You have to have respect for that kind of mourning, too. You can't just say, *You're a bad person because you were part of all this inhumanity.*

"There a part of my nature that's compassionate," Gaby continued. "To teach people and not turn them off, you have to use more of that compassionate part of your nature. It's easy to be angry; it's easy to lash out. It's so much harder to use your intellect to think in a compassionate way how to teach somebody or influence somebody to change what they're doing." When Gaby thinks back on the teachers who were unkind to her, she wonders if they hated Native people or if they really thought they were doing the right thing, perhaps acting from a "save the man, kill the Indian" attitude. By understanding how we're all connected, feeling empathy for your "enemies" allows you to do the hard work of challenging injustice without damaging your own spirit through rage.

From her grandmothers, Gaby learned that you have to resist the idea that what you know as an indigenous person is not valued. "Don't be mean to Europeans," they cautioned, "but you can't trust their thinking, either." When the Mormons knocked on her grandmother's door, she refused to talk with them. She said, "Europeans have been here for two hundred years, and they haven't learned a single thing. They are not listening."

"Where did the idea come from that older cultures don't have wisdom that's worth listening to?" Gaby mused. "We need to learn from that old culture and adapt it to today. For example, it's very much a Dakota belief that it's easier to keep the land pristine than to muck it up and have to fix it later. That concept is at the core of ancestral ecological knowledge."

In a 2011 *Circle* newspaper article about a film created from the Dakota 38 Memorial Ride, codirector Sarah Weston, from Flandreau, said that one of the film's messages is that Dakota people "should take a simple but difficult step: forgive the misdeeds of the past."

The trouble with making sweeping recommendations like that, Gaby said, is that "pain has its own timetable. You can't rush it. You can't forgive somebody before you're ready. You can't tell anybody else how to reach that point. You can just say, *This is what I did; maybe it will help them with their experience.* Everybody has their own path through those dreadful, heartbreaking times in their lives.

"Mainstream society can't grasp the meaning of historical trauma," Gaby explained, "because they don't know the human face on it." One of the young men who was part of the Ride committed suicide, unable to find a way out of his grief and depression. The young man, Billy DuMarce, is the face of that story.

When Gaby talks about reparations for the past, what she means is concrete programs that help people like Billy DuMarce deal with issues that are the result of generations suffering from historical trauma. Where are the psychiatrists if the suicide rate is so high? Where are the schools if people aren't graduating? Instead we have politicians introducing legislation to eliminate the Bureau of Indian Affairs and funding for Native health programs. We have people making plans to develop the area around Historic Fort Snelling but excluding participation by Dakota people and disregarding its significance for Dakota people as both a sacred site and a place where atrocities were committed.

Gestures of reconciliation are being made. People in Redwood Falls, a town that was part of the 1862 Dakota War, are working with Dakota elders to rename Ramsey Park, named for the governor who famously said, "Sioux Indians must be exterminated or driven forever beyond the borders of the state." A Minnesota legislator wants to repeal the federal law that exiled Dakota people from Minnesota. In 2010, the Tribal Law and Order Act was passed to protect Native women from a disproportionately high level of sexual assault, primarily by non-Native men. Even small gestures can begin to educate people and increase their awareness of what remains to be done to provide justice for Dakota people.

To maintain her strength and balance in a struggle that will undoubtedly continue into future generations, Gaby turns to spiritual events like the Dakota Commemorative March and the Dakota 38 Memorial Ride. Without contemplative time spent in solitude and prayer, she risks traumatizing her spirit.

"Horses have had a healing power for me and my family," Gaby said. "I have an appreciation for horses because of how it helped Hunter to heal. It's going to help the tribe heal. We have that importance of the horse as a horse culture. I used something that our ancestors used to try and help my son. There are subtleties there that if you're open to observing, they can really help. But someone has to teach that to you. You have to have those seeds planted. Those are the things that are available to you in life to help you get through the really tough moments."

For Gaby, that means continuing to do her artwork and her writing: "I really believe it's important to tell the story so that the important things that happened don't fade away. Memory needs to speak up. Artwork has been such an important part of my life, validating who I am in spite of larger society saying, *You're not worth anything.* I could communicate ideas. When I dance, you can really feel the earth through the moccasins. There are qualities of strength that you get from making those connections. It really takes observing your world and being sensitive to everything you feel. The danger of being such a sensitive person is that you don't have the resilience to fight injustice. It's a really hard thing to balance so that you don't become overwhelmed by sorrow."

When Gaby is riding her horse alongside the Minnesota River or walking on roads that were once trails made by Dakota relatives, she wonders if the land itself misses seeing Dakota people: "Does it miss hearing our prayer songs and seeing the eagle feather staff? Sometimes when eagles hover over us on the walk and on the ride, are they saying they're glad to see us back again?" When you see how scarred and unkempt the land has been allowed to become, she wonders if the earth wants us back.

"If you think of the thousands of years we've been on this landscape, this hard period is really short," Gaby said. "It's probably the blink of an eye for the earth. When we sing those prayer songs, we're singing the people back to our homeland."

Delores Brunelle and Dolton

Delores Brunelle

As we rounded the corner on a deserted road, I was scanning the woods for the red gleam of high-bush cranberries when Delores gently touched my arm. She said, "Look." About two hundred yards ahead of us, three wolves stood in the middle of the road. They stared back at us without moving, watching our slow approach. We waited in silence, hardly breathing, to see what they would do next. After a long moment of scrutiny, they turned back in the direction they had come, disappearing into the trees. Two black wolves and one gray, with long legs and powerful bodies. My first wolf sighting.

We drove farther, at last reaching the narrow road that was little more than two dirt tracks through tall grass. We parked, gathered our bags and tools, and stood admiring the thick stand of ripe chokecherry trees in front of us. Delores offered me her tobacco pouch. Holding a pinch in my left hand, I listened as she offered a prayer to the elder of the trees, giving thanks for its gifts. After releasing our tobacco at its foot, we moved on. We would not gather berries from the tree where we prayed.

Chokecherry trees grow in abundance at the south edge of this forest, seeking the full afternoon sunlight that falls between deep woods and open field. Delores and her grandson, Dolton, knew these woods well, knew where to find the chokecherries that were ready to be picked. Each

Delores and Dolton have chosen to change their names to protect Dolton's privacy while still sharing their story. No other details have been altered.

of us carried a cotton bag over our shoulder. I had learned from earlier visits with Delores to pick a third or less of the fruit on a tree. We were not here to strip the trees bare, to regard all that we found as belonging to us. We were only one of the creatures that needed the fruit to survive, sharing it with birds, insects, and bears. Instead, we spread our picking across a broad area, moving from one stand to the next, always leaving plenty behind. Often we had to push through thick underbrush and tall weeds to reach the next tree. We wore pants and long sleeves against the mosquitoes rather than using chemical sprays.

Picking berries in late summer when the sunlight has begun to soften, when the sumac bushes are already turning a brilliant scarlet, is a tradition that has been shared by many generations of Native women. Not only were we gathering a valuable food for the fall and winter, we were sharing quiet hours in the woods and long grass, a companionable silence falling between us.

Dolton picked for a short time and then ran through the weeds, hiding behind trees and stumps, popping up in surprise. He wore an orange nylon gathering bag tied at his hip. Rather than burying his head in a video game while we drove, he chattered and pointed at berry bushes along the side of the road. Earlier that morning, he had declared, "I'm a student of my grandma," and then went back to his endless sorting of Pokemon cards. Dolton was already adept at identifying chokecherries, blueberries, rose hips, and high-bush cranberries, offering warm berries on his brown palm as a sample for guests.

He was a happy boy in the woods, leaving behind all the cares of his complicated short life. At nine years old, he had chosen to live with his grandmother and yet still needed to grieve for his absent family, who are unable to care for him. But today, on this warm September afternoon, when we have already seen three wolves and filled our bags with berries to be made into syrup and jam, today was a perfect day.

A short distance from where I stood plucking berries with fingers stained wine red, I could see Delores moving deliberately around branches laden with ripe fruit. Still recovering from knee surgery, she moved slowly and carefully, especially on uneven ground obscured by weeds. She too glowed this afternoon, the sun catching her silver hair, her face beaming with pleasure at picking berries with a friend. Here, surrounded by endless acres of trees and few people, Delores's intensity was softened, her relentless inquiry was at peace. Here, in the wilds of the northern Minnesota forest, she was in a state of grace.

At sixty-two, living on forty acres of family land an hour northwest of Duluth, Delores is raising her grandson in a small one-bedroom house. The rooms are meticulously arranged with an artist's eye for color, texture, and function. She maintains a tobacco fire in the yard, opening a circle of trust around her house. Shortly after she first moved here, she fell asleep outside in her chair with a bowl of grapes on the table next to her. When she woke, the grapes were gone. She could see fox tracks and the indentation where the fox had been lying not far from her chair. Since then, Delores and Dolton have known six generations of fox pups that have grown up near the house. Sometimes an owl will come and spend the day, or even several weeks, perched on the standing dead tree visible from her window. Other times a marten comes and eats at the bird feeder. Deer pass through; a wolf and many different kinds of birds come in search of food. She reads the scat left behind to know who has visited during the night.

Delores is still recovering from a brain injury she suffered several years earlier while working as an art therapist at Circle of Nations Wahpeton Indian School, an off-reservation boarding school located in Wahpeton, North Dakota. She bent down to pick up her dropped keys just before a student slammed open a steel door, not realizing she was behind it. Her condition, which is not apparent to a casual acquaintance, drains her energy with seizures and disorientation. Yet when Dolton came to visit in the summer and asked to stay, she did not hesitate. Delores was awarded custody of Dolton years earlier when his mother was unable to care for him because of her addictions. Even at nine, he knows that he is safe with her.

In the old days, Dakota grandparents were revered as the keepers of tribal traditions and spent time with their grandchildren teaching kinship terms, duties owed to various relatives, stories, and family history and in general providing unequivocal love and acceptance. Grandparents who helped raise their grandchildren freed the mothers to gather food and provide for their families. Generations of Native people who were raised in boarding schools grew up separated from their families and often did not learn the skills needed to parent their own children. Falling back on their traditional role within the *tiyospaye*, or extended family, many grandparents are filling in as parents while their children deal with personal crises.

Grandmothers, like Delores, find themselves raising children with little money or energy, nearly 19 percent of them living in poverty. Delores lives on disability, an income that is not enough for two people. She rises at 5:30 to help Dolton get ready for school. She helps him with his homework, makes costumes for school events, meets with his teacher. Twice a week they drive to judo, coming home at 9:30. They drive to his therapist in Duluth, a fifty-five-mile trip.

Once the decision was made, Dolton quickly settled into a new school, his sweet personality winning him new friends. But his heart longs for love from his mother and from the family he had been living with, whose methods of punishment were physical and demeaning. Dolton turns his anger first on himself—*If I weren't a bad boy, then they would love me*—and then on Delores: *This is all your fault.* He lashes out with angry words, resents his life, his loneliness, his loss. Delores is patient, calmly corrects his challenge that she does not love him either. She waits until his anger is spent, patiently guiding him through the ordinary steps of his day, creating a safe structure of meals, homework, bath, and bedtime that contains his anger. At last he winds down, spent of emotion, and slumps into Delores's arms, wordless, a displaced boy with a broken heart.

At times the challenge is almost more than she can bear. Dolton's tantrums, his immense neediness, have awakened her own memories of abandonment as a child, her own outrage at feeling violated, unprotected, and unloved. As he storms, she is both his loving grandmother and a vulnerable child; she feels his loneliness and pain with an ache that has never been healed. She can see his angry defiance for what it is: the torment of a traumatized boy. She creates a safe place where he is cherished and protected, where he is both allowed to feel his anger and contained within the boundary of mutual respect. While his volatile emotions fluctuate, the consistent structure of his day reinforces his innate goodness, his worth as a human being.

"He's a prince," Delores said, meaning it with her whole heart. Dolton is an exceptional child who has survived more than many adults. He has retained, with Delores's support, a loving spirit. In opening her life and home to Dolton, in witnessing his pain and reengaging with her own, she heals them both by offering to him what he needs, what she too needed as a child.

In the summer, Delores sets up a large tent in the yard where they both sleep at night. Handmade quilts cover two cots with a wide rug in between, creating a small living room where they fall asleep listening to the wind, to the not-so-distant howl of a wolf, and watch the faint glow of northern lights through the thin shell of the tent. When his mother calls from a treatment facility as part of the supervised phone calls that Delores has arranged, Dolton tells her about this magical outdoor room. Later that night, the police knock on Delores's door. Child protection has received a report that Dolton is at risk, sleeping outside near wolves. A policeman walks through her house with a flashlight. Delores asks him not to wake Dolton. He asks what is going on. She tells him, drug addiction. He leaves.

Delores says that she is the one in her family who will not tolerate the generations-old dysfunction. Her family has turned against her, shut her out completely, regarding her as not loyal. Dolton is in his own pre-adolescent turmoil, encouraged by several family members to find fault with Delores. He tells her, "You're always in a bad mood. You don't want to do anything!"

She sits next to him on the couch and says gently, "What about saying, *Thanks, Grandma, for coloring with me this morning*? Or, *Thank you, Grandma, for making chokecherry syrup with me this morning.*"

As he listens, his anger calms. He says, "Thank you, Grandma, for the way you giggle when something is funny." They sit together until his resistance fades, until the pattern he has unconsciously adopted melts away, until he is once again a vulnerable nine-year-old boy. He stays close to Delores's side, not wanting to leave her for a moment.

Raising Dolton has changed the ease of their relationship as grandmother and grandchild. Dolton once said to Delores, "Now that you're my parent, I miss being with you as my grandma."

When he used to stay for six-month visits, they spent their time working in the garden, singing songs, and gathering plants and berries in the woods. Delores said, "Whenever he was with me, we were finding ways to be connected to the Great Mystery."

Delores is also passing on the gift that her grandfather gave when he recognized in her a child who was open to being taught about the unseen world. Dakota elders would also observe the inherent nature in a child in order to support and mentor his or her unique gifts and identity. Delores has recognized in Dolton an intuitive grasp and willingness to be part of his own healing process as a "student of my grandmother." Dolton has already received his name, participated in a healing ceremony for his mother, and "welcomed to the circle" in a formal ceremony.

In his younger years, Delores enjoyed her grandson without the weight of parental responsibility, the many decisions to be made with regard to school, friends, activities.

When Delores is invited or asked to serve on committees for school or in the community, she declines. The fatigue of raising a child as a single parent drains all of her energy. She says, "I am contributing by raising an individual who will become a responsible member of the community." While there is no hesitation, no regret in her decision to resume custody of Dolton, she must deal with an ongoing struggle to balance her own health with his needs.

Yet Dolton's presence in her life, while exhausting, is also renewing, giving her the opportunity to apply all that she has learned in her life about healing from trauma. Looking back on raising her two children as a single parent, she knows that she was not able to give them what she can now offer to Dolton: a depth of understanding around healing from generations of family dysfunction. For her, the grief comes in knowing that while she can help Dolton grow into a responsible, loving adult, the understanding has come too late to help her own kids.

I met Delores in 2006 when a group of ten Native women gathered for the first time at the Dream of Wild Health farm in Hugo, Minnesota. The founder, Sally Auger, had invited us to be part of a women's circle that would commit to relearning traditional ways of cooking and working with food and medicinal plants. With the farm's focus on providing healthy indigenous foods to the Native community, Sally knew how important it was to work with the women who often do much of the cooking within the family. From her experience working with Native people in recovery, Sally also understood the deep connection between the food we eat, the time we spend tending the earth, and healing from historical trauma. The women were Dakota, Lakota, Ojibwe, and sometimes a mix; we shared an interest in rediscovering the foods of our ancestors, albeit using contemporary cooking methods. Sometimes, when we could not ask a traditionally trained cook, that meant Googling a recipe, which made us laugh.

On a Saturday morning in late fall, we sat around a long kitchen table with sunlight streaming in through the windows. Outside, a blanket of yellow leaves covered the ground. We began with each woman sharing her name and something of her background. I met Donna LaChapelle, an Ojibwe/Dakota grandmother, who later became the program manager and adopted mother for the kids at the farm, nurturing, loving, and always pushing them to do their best. She brought her friend of many years Delores Brunelle, who introduced herself as Ojibwe, enrolled at White Earth, and then sang a sweet song that she and her grandson, Dolton, had composed about their garden.

During the break, I asked Delores a question about her grandmother, whom she had mentioned briefly. She did not respond for a long moment, holding the full force of her gaze on me. I could see she had turned inward, not really seeing me any longer.

She spoke finally, briefly, about having lived with her grandmother and enduring her abuse, her emotional instability. It was my first glimpse of the pain that Delores lived with and the beginning of a friendship based on a mutual interest in recognizing and healing from trauma.

This shared interest has helped me see how trauma affects Native people across tribal boundaries as well as the possibilities for working together and learning from each other. While it is essential to retain the unique language, stories, history, and traditions of each tribe, historical trauma has wounded Native people in ways that we share as human beings. Delores's lifetime experience with her family's dysfunction, as well as working with Native youth from many tribes, including Dakota, has taught her firsthand how to deal with diverse communities on the complex issues of colonization.

Contrary to the belief that the Dakota and Ojibwe were constantly at war, our work together reaffirms the friendly relations that existed between tribes, including many intermarriages. We also have a history of learning from each other. A Dakota woman, Tail Feather Woman, received a vision of the Big Drum that was first brought to the Ojibwe in northern Minnesota. She passed on the vision along with the songs and protocols for the ceremony, which still exists today with many Big Drum Societies.

Although Delores was forced into early retirement by her brain injury, she has devoted much of her life to working with intergenerational trauma. She was born in 1946 in South St. Paul, but her relatives lived on the Leech Lake Reservation, subsisting on hunting, fishing, and gardening. They had a reverence for the tools of survival; everything was made beautiful. Delores's mother, who had attended boarding school in Red Lake, preferred to "pass" as French Canadian, spending hours styling her hair and makeup to resemble Elizabeth Taylor. Delores's father came from a family of musicians who farmed in Nebraska, living in sod huts until the Dust Bowl wiped them out. Her father found work at the Civilian Conservation Corps lumber camps in Ely, Minnesota, where he met his future wife's family. He used to sing melancholy songs that Delores learned as a child, music she recognized later as a form of storytelling.

Delores's grandfather was a highly respected herbalist at Leech Lake, a healer whose "equanimity and regard for people was uncompromising."

When she was five, he began teaching her about plants as well as some of the profound and yet basic truths about how healing happens through communion. As a young child, Delores would lie down on her stomach, heart to heart with the earth, and fall into a deep sleep, waking up in a "state of communion" with the plants and trees around her.

"No matter who I met, plant, animal, bug or bird, I asked, *Who are you and what is my relationship to you?*" Delores said. "That's my Native identity. I don't believe that I would be alive without that piece. It gave me a focus, turned my face toward beauty in the midst of heinous treatment toward children." She explained that when we sit with plants, when we establish a relationship, we can be a witness to the "Kind-Hearted Great Mystery." During years of enduring physical and emotional abuse as a child, "the unseen world, the plant nation, stood by me every step of the way. They administer to us exactly where we are. They offer us abundant compassion and unconditional acceptance."

When she was nine years old, Delores discovered a 35-millimeter camera in her parents' closet. She taught herself how to use it and began photographing her "ordinary amazing life, on the water and in the woods of northern Minnesota" when they visited her relatives.

After high school, her gift as an artist won her a scholarship to the Rhode Island School of Design. Unable to afford more than the free first semester, Delores returned to Minnesota, intending to study at the Minneapolis College of Art and Design. Her interest in learning a creative process that had more spiritual depth than the Western approach, with its emphasis on technique, turned her life in a new direction. She was drawn to the teachings of Rabindranath Tagore—whose book *Gitanjali* won the Nobel Prize for Literature in 1913—and the belief that an image should be created so that a person's soul would rise up and excel in his or her humanity: "There is only your own pair of wings and the pathless sky./Bird, o my bird, listen to me, do not close your wings." Delores was so entranced by Tagore's teachings that she signed up for three months in a student exchange program in India, wanting "to go where he breathed the air." She brought her camera and began to immerse herself in photographing the world.

Within a few years, her photography began to gain attention, winning her a Rockefeller Grant to document the ceremonial cycle at the Crow Agency in Montana and exhibitions in New York City. After a failed marriage left her with two young children to raise, she returned to school for a degree in elementary education from Hamline University in St. Paul. Her drawing instructor urged her to enroll in art therapy at the University of Wisconsin–Superior, a program that combined her interests in healing and the creative process. Delores insisted on tailoring the program to her Native identity by working with an elder, Murphy Jackson. As Delores explored the use of image from an indigenous perspective, Murphy helped her find the language to describe her process. "He would listen, listen, listen and then put his hand on mine and say, *It's time for you to start working with cedar.* I had to figure out how to go into a deep, disciplined relationship with cedar," Delores said.

Finally, despite her achievements, Delores could no longer ignore her deteriorating health, the constant anxiety and panic attacks that were depleting her energy. Years of raising two children as a single parent while working toward her master's degree had brought her to a state of complete exhaustion. Murphy told her, "You are not made for this. Working your mind this hard for so long has thrown you out of balance. You were made to live a quiet life." With only a few months left in her program, Delores went on to complete her degree.

During the three years of intense instruction with Murphy, through her own discipline of dreaming and visioning, Delores was given a creative process for inquiry—Becoming Human Spontaneously—that would become her life work. Her gift is an ability to facilitate another person in witnessing their self making the journey to conception, when we are "becoming human spontaneously." This journey includes color, rhythm, sound, light, and awareness, qualities and attributes that were present before the body formed. The process of perceiving these attributes is not analytical; it involves direct perception, or "bookless learning." Part of this work is also an intuitive process for developing relationships with plants by closing your eyes, listening deeply to your own longing, and perceiving the plant that responds.

Before leaving for New Mexico to work for the Eight Northern Pueblos, Delores devoted a year to making giveaway items for a ceremony. When she was ready, she committed her whole heart to ending the patterns of intergenerational abuse in her family. "I want this body to be the place where they are transmuted," Delores said. "I want it to happen here and not go into future generations. The generations before me, I want them to have relief. I want to be shaped into a person who loves the people who harmed me as much as I love the people who love me."

In New Mexico, Delores encountered many challenges that would test her commitment. When a work environment became hostile and she wanted to quit, Murphy said, "No, you asked for this. This man's soul needs what you want to become. Every day you need to sit down and find the deepest, purest chamber in your heart and send to him from there." He told her, "You'll know when you're done." After two years of daily practice, Delores experienced a vivid dream that told her she was done.

The Indian Health Service also recruited Delores to work in an adolescent treatment center at the Acoma Pueblo. Some of teens she worked with had been recruited by satanists. Finally, they told her, "What you learned in training won't help. Hear our story instead." Delores agreed, entering into their dark world in order to understand why they joined.

"I went home every night and threw up," Delores said. What she learned was that the unspeakable acts committed by these children were motivated by a desire to create a better world. They had been promised anarchy, the destruction of the greedy, materialistic world we live in.

One student challenged her under the American Indian Religious Freedom Act to be allowed to create images of satanic altars. Delores agreed, provided he would allow equal time for her process, learning how to perceive himself through the eyes of the Kind-Hearted Great Mystery. After ridiculing her request as gross, stupid, and sentimental, he agreed. As part of Delores's curriculum, students were also required to "allow yourselves to be seen by first light," two hours before dawn. After three months of painting his satanic altars and parents on a funeral pyre, the youth showed up with a tender painting of himself on a mesa at first light, blending violets and blues to show the wind as it moved across the earth, plants bending in response. He said, *Dear God, I'm willing to see myself through your eyes.*

Delores's curriculum was attracting a great deal of interest in the academic world. She was hired by well-known author Greg Cajete to work at the Institute of American Indian Arts (IAIA), where she taught Native philosophy as a creative process of inquiry and Native American social psychology. She assigned her students to research how their living grandparents had experienced colonization. One student said that when he asked his grandmother the first question, she began to cry, saying she didn't think anybody cared.

At the same time, the University of New Mexico hired Delores to teach cross-cultural art therapy to white graduate students so they would understand colonization as the origin of the trauma that was being labeled as mental illness in therapy. She was also hired by the Santa Fe Indian School to work with high-risk Native youth. She taught them to listen to the images they created as "the voice of the ancestral world pouring through each of you" and to witness each drawing as a "doorway to the unseen world."

For teens who had already endured hard experiences within their own families, this approach was not always immediately accepted. They would ask, "How does this work help me?"

Delores would reply, "You've lived your life without feeling valued. What you get here is the sense that you are loved. In the eyes of your ancestors, and in the eyes of the natural world, you are valuable, unique, cherished."

After three years, Delores remarried and relocated to Shiprock, New Mexico, where she found herself struggling in the midst of her husband's dysfunctional family. After several years of continuing her work teaching, presenting at conferences, and working as a contractor in Native organizations addressing conflict resolution and racism, her health began to fail again. She left her marriage, spent two years in Albuquerque working and studying ayurveda with Dr. Vasant Lad, and returned home to Minnesota. In the fall of 2000, she was recruited by the Circle of Nations boarding school in Wahpeton, North Dakota, to work as an art therapist with youth who were dealing with severe trauma in their homes. The following spring, she dropped her keys at the exact moment that a steel door would literally propel her into the next stage of her life. At the moment of impact, Delores saw the same dream turtle that had appeared in her life every time she needed to leave a situation.

A year after we met at the farm, I turned down the gravel road that leads to Delores's driveway, watching for the red metal gate that was standing open for my arrival. I unloaded the car, and we left immediately for a long walk. We passed the neat rows of vegetables in her garden, the squash just now blooming after a late planting, unlikely to bear fruit this year. Balsam trees that filled in after the virgin forest was clear-cut framed her extensive yard. As we walked, she showed me where we would gather swamp tea the next day, the same place where she used to gather plants with her dad when she was a young woman.

We returned home in the starlit dusk and shared a light meal of salad greens from her garden, garnished with radishes, nuts, raisins, and a home-made dressing. Afterward, we sat with cups of warm swamp tea, a light fragrant beverage that is soothing to the nervous system.

"The core message of colonization," Delores began, "is that Native people are not valued. This message has been directed toward every aspect of Native culture, from spirituality to our indigenous diet." After generations of brutal, systematic repression have left a wake of identity confusion, low self-esteem, and epidemic levels of disease and dysfunction, we are beginning to see this message as pervasive throughout our society. Yet to make societal change, each one of us has to look at the ways we have internalized it, altering the way we raise our children, relate to our partners, and define our priorities. We must take responsibility for our own lives, becoming mindful of our own distortions.

One way to begin is by bringing our attention back to the body. By simply observing how we respond to situations, how we resist experiencing our own pain, we can see the physical effects of trauma. The body has its own intelligence, a distinct, visceral witnessing that accepts everything that happens, incorporates it, and knows how to release it, given the mind's cooperation. Our survival as indigenous people relied on our ability to be intensely present in each moment. As Dr. Brave Heart pointed out, we had ceremonies and teachings that helped us accept and release painful experiences. When this release was blocked for the generations that endured the initial deep trauma, we became disconnected from our emotions and our bodies. In relearning mindfulness, we recover an indigenous awareness that pays attention to everything around and within us.

This state of mindfulness was woven into all aspects of indigenous life, just as appreciation for creative expression and beauty was present in ordinary tools and practical items. Activities like berry picking were not only a means of gathering food; they were also moments of communion, experiencing the reciprocity of giving and receiving with a plant. When we are silent, contemplative, filled with a loving regard for everything around us, we enter into communion with the earth as our mother. Restoring this connection as a daily practice helps us move from the mind back to the heart, reestablishing balance between the body, mind, spirit, and emotions. "Being in relationship with all other orders of life," Delores said, "is fundamental to Native culture because it keeps the heart open." Cultural genocide, the forced assimilation of our people, has interrupted the silence we once cultivated, disrupted the practice of daily communion, and substituted coping with life in a noise-filled, fragmented, and unsafe world.

"I didn't understand when I was growing up that daily practice of gathering and communion would create the kind of being that I was wanting to become," Delores said. "If you have a longing, that's your original self asking you to cooperate in becoming who you are. Or it's your ancestors asking you to help so that life experiences they couldn't resolve would be resolved."

A friend of Delores's once said to her, "If Indians hadn't gotten so involved with alcohol, they would have been able to heal from the effects of colonization." She shook her head in disbelief as she told me the story. Alcohol was originally introduced to Native people by European traders who used it as a bargaining tool and a means of manipulating both trade deals and treaty negotiations. After generations had endured loss that is unimaginable today, alcohol became first a refuge from pain that is literally unbearable and ultimately a physical addiction. The stereotype of drunken Indians suggests an inherent weakness of character and prevents people from seeing, understanding, and knowing the joy and beauty of original Native lifeways. The beauty of Native culture has been masked by trauma, oppression, and the legacy of cultural genocide.

The next morning was bright and cold with a forewarning of early fall. We strapped light cotton gathering bags across our chests, tucked folded knives in our pockets. Wildflowers still bloomed in abundance along both sides of the road, a mix of asters, swamp milkweed, goldenrod, and many other plants whose names I did not know. As we walked, Delores explained how wild plants choose where they grow, bringing to the surface minerals that cannot be accessed through a garden. "But gathering wild food is not just about nutrition," she added. "Just as important, gathering is also necessary for psychological health and spiritual development. Developing a relationship with the plant nation requires a paradigm shift."

In other words, you can become "Native" by learning how to live on and listen to the land where you are placed. You allow the land to provide for you and to teach you. "That's *being* Native," Delores said, "when you're not just Native in your head." Eating Native means eating nutrient-rich wild plants that are indigenous to the area, reestablishing a lifeway in which you pay attention to the plants that grow around you, following the seasons. The fruits of some plants are harvested in one season; the leaves, stem, or root may be harvested in another. Some plants are harvested with dew; others are not. The cycles of the moon also make a difference, especially for medicinal plants. "Plants manifest light into life," Delores said, quoting Dr. Vasant Lad from *The Yoga of Herbs*. "And humans transform life into consciousness."

Eating local, on the other hand, is more of a political statement about eating foods that have less dependence on carbon-based fuels to bring them to the table. These tend to be cultivated plants, like the carrot, that are grown within a fifty-mile radius of where you live. Dream of Wild Health raises both organic vegetables like carrots, green beans, and eggplant as well as indigenous foods like the Three Sisters. Cultivated foods rich in nutrients can be an important part of the diet, especially when grown from heirloom seeds that are preserved within tribes and families.

Delores believes that the indigenous way of living belongs to all, that it is our birthright as human beings. Returning to it, however, requires tremendous discipline, especially while overcoming the effects of intergenerational trauma. People have stopped listening to their longing in part because it carries so much discipline and responsibility, qualities that are not compatible with a lifestyle of coping with unresolved trauma or with the values of a materialistic society. And then there's the question of the chicken and the egg: do we begin working with the effects and symptoms of trauma or do we go straight to relearning the spiritual practices and values that have been displaced? In other words, do we need to understand our genocidal history first?

Either way, enormous effort is required to witness an emotional wound that has been absorbed into one's body and mind, to drain it of its toxicity, revealing itself as a teacher and thereby transforming what was a painful wound into personal growth. We can do this if we hold to spiritual discipline rather than identifying ourselves as the pain. Delores said, "When I die, I want to be resolved enough that when my body goes into the earth, it generates medicine plants."

As a former trainer with the National Association for Native American Children of Alcoholics (NANACOA) team, Delores facilitated groups in week-long intensive sessions dealing with intergenerational trauma, much of it stemming from boarding schools. Her work helped counter the perception that Native people are "bad," challenging the shame that is internalized by teaching people to reach deep into their essential selves, the innate beings that prevail even in the presence of trauma. This work recognizes the tendency of the mind to resist change, creating a veil, offering up a little piece of resolution that does little to change the genetic imprint of intergenerational trauma. To change the DNA, one must go deeper.

When the effects of any trauma are not resolved in one generation, Delores explained, the next generation inherits the trauma of the previous generation: "Returning to ceremonial cycle, rebuilding healthy families and communities, restoring our relationship with the natural world while celebrating the beauty of who we are; these are additional necessary elements of complete recovery, and the aspects are the *traditional domain of tribal life* . . . An important and effective first step in our recovery is the telling of our story, individually and collectively."

A few days before her mother passed away, Delores worked with her therapist and finally reached an understanding of the original imprint, the message or lesson or teaching that has formed the core of her family's dysfunction. Delores's mother attended boarding school in Red Lake, and her grandmother attended Pipestone Indian School. Over the years, thousands of Native children have learned the message that is implicit in boarding school education: that Native people are children of the devil who are condemned by God. This sense of worthlessness, of evil, of unlovability *because* they were Native was turned inward, internalized, becoming the root for some of the profound dysfunction later in life.

What makes this message so difficult to change is that these imprints are beyond the reach of the conscious mind because they often extend across generations, making access nearly impossible except as inherited trauma. Children like Delores inherit the sense that they are evil along with the repressed grief at being seen that way by God, by the Creator, by the Great Mystery that surrounds us.

When Dolton chose to return and live with her, Delores honored her commitment to stop the patterns of dysfunction inherited from her family and passed on to her children. She didn't realize how far that commitment would need to go or where it would ultimately take her. Delores has invested a lifetime of working with spiritual leaders in the Native community, combined with a disciplined practice in many other modalities of therapy and healing, including ayurveda and mindfulness. These teachings

offered insight and at least temporary comfort and refuge from the patterns within her family, slowly addressing the issue of trauma by approaching it from every possible angle. "You start by building a cognitive life raft,"
Delores said. "All of the affirmations, the different modalities of therapy
and healing, are all necessary parts of a complex process. You address every
angle of the issue until you get to the bottom-line imprint."

Ironically, it was the head injury she received that has supported much
of her recovery process. While at Wahpeton, she worked with kids from
White Earth, Fort Totten, and Red Lake, all of the places that her family
members had attended. When she was injured, it was the school's insur-
ance that provided the therapy that opened up her process to perceive
the original imprint, the message that had so twisted her family's ability to
love and to function. A few days after Delores received this understanding,
her mother passed away. "And yet she remains," Delores said, "as a partner
in this work."

"Releasing this imprint is possible," Delores said, "when you can feel
gratitude for the truth at the core of the experience." While this may seem
shocking and incomprehensible at first, the practice of attending to our
suffering through mindfulness takes us into the heart of the trauma experience where we witness our original innocence. We realize that nothing
has been lost; we are whole. When our original self is freed from painful
distortions, we can feel gratitude and compassion, and forgiveness becomes possible. From this understanding, righteous indignation can grow
free of bitterness, vengeance, and resentment. We can demand justice without rewounding ourselves.

Later, as Delores absorbed the full impact of what it meant for thousands of innocent Native children to be taught this lesson in boarding
school, she wept. Through this process, she has moved from the defensive-
ness that has dominated her life to forgiveness for what she has projected,
forgiving her own brokenness and becoming "a profound listener who can
have a compassionate, considered response" to the world.

As parents, we all struggle with the legacies within our families that
we have inherited, and in that struggle we pass on some portion of those

legacies to our children. But if we do transformative work in our own lifetime, then we may have the opportunity to give our grandchildren the
benefit of what we have learned and to make amends with our children.

And yet we resist making change. As elder Earl Day said, "It's like going
to a powwow. Sometimes people say, *I don't feel well; I can't go.* But the
healing they need is at the powwow." I learned this lesson when I called
Delores's house one morning to explain that I would need to leave early
from a Wild Gathering weekend: about a dozen people were coming to
work with Earl and Delores in the woods. This weekend was the culmination of Delores's dream to bring together a group of Native and non-Native
people who share her commitment to traditional lifeways like gathering
wild plants to use as food and medicine. I explained my heavy workload,
my need to return to the Cities a day early to prepare for my deadlines, my
stress from overwork.

Delores listened to me complain without comment. Then she said,
"You know how important it is to come on time and stay until the end of
an event. The healing for the stress will come during this weekend, and
commitment is an important aspect of the work." She explained the difference between degenerative pain, as in patterns of chronic overwork in
understaffed organizations, and regenerative pain, as in the discomfort
of committing the time to the weekend even though it would mean less
time to work. She described my state of mind as characterized by "dogged
obedience," an insistence on perfect completion of a commitment to a
degenerative environment. By leaving early, I was sacrificing the healing
opportunity in this weekend for the sake of maintaining chronic patterns.

I had to admit that in my work, I tend to run full speed ahead until I run
right over the edge of a cliff and hang there for a moment, suspended in car-
toon time, realizing belatedly that I, like the coyote, will soon crash on the
canyon floor. But when I told Delores that I had gone over the cliff and was
about to fall, she said, "Then fly." I stayed for the entire weekend, admitting
that she was right. Since patterns are hard to change, however, I continued
to use this excuse at other events. Then she would remind me, "You're
lucky to have me as a friend who will challenge you to learn this principle."

In speaking so bluntly, Delores also demonstrated the power of truth telling as a rigorous practice, from the small moments in our daily lives to the work of challenging institutionalized racism and colonization. Unlike the rage that comes from repressing the truth, truth telling is an act of defense, of standing up for yourself as someone who is neither bully nor victim. Speaking the truth does not mean just being critical; it requires a balanced state of mind, a detached *presence* capable of both clarity and compassion. The challenge lies in first seeing the truth when all of our minds have been colonized.

Delores woke one morning after Dolton had come to live with her and felt the full force of her resistance to raising a nine-year-old child at the age of sixty-two. The feeling swelled to a clamor, raising her heart rate, sending electrical sparks down her arms, laying a weight on her limbs until they became almost too heavy to move. She wept, in mourning for all the pain and grief she had known in her life that had brought her to the decision to keep Dolton. Only by staying with the feeling, by accepting all of its aspects in an act of *passive witnessing awareness,* could she transform what would be one of the great challenges in her life to a loving experience filled with grace. As Delores knows all too well, it's easy to repeat patterns in difficult family relationships. The key is to transform the experience from the inside.

This process has helped Delores "move from the person who was not there for my kids to being the person who is there for my grandson." With this understanding, however, comes immense grief for the pain experienced by her children growing up in a dysfunctional family. She has needed a lifetime to transform her own childhood into emotional work that is restorative rather than degenerative pain.

Several months later, on a weekend in January that was typically one of the coldest weeks of the year, we stood at the foot of a path that led straight into the woods, rose to a peak, and then disappeared. The snow was untouched by the unseasonal rain that fell farther south and turned roads into skating rinks. We could see a few sparse footsteps from earlier travelers. In the spring and summer, this path is a narrow road, two dirt tracks separated by tall grasses and wild plants.

We wore snowshoes to navigate the deep snow. Dolton walked at the side of the trail where there was no path. I had the advantage of a semi-broken trail ahead of me, partially compacted snow that made a more level base for my snowshoes. Dolton was delighted when his snowshoes completely disappeared from sight, sinking below the surface of the snow, rendering him a footless ten-year-old boy. Then he broke into a run, raising his heels high behind him and churning a white cloud of snow until he was barely visible. He stopped, his body hung for a moment motionless, and then he toppled to the side of the path, allowing the snow to break his fall. He lay there frozen, not moving. I plodded past him, admired his still form, his arms spread like an angel in the snow. Behind us Delores made her slow but insistent way up the hill. At the crest, I suggested to her that we turn back. I was thinking about her damaged knee, her lack of strength. She said, "No, let's keep going. We'll just pace ourselves."

The path was a narrow clearing through dense woods, white spruce and poplars that towered over us on either side. We were searching for the cedar trees where Delores had gathered in a warmer season. We moved slowly, with care. There was no reason to rush. It was a rare day—a temperature perfect for strenuous exercise, fresh snow, bright sky arching beyond the tips of evergreens. The glare of sun on white snow was softened by the blue shadows of the woods around us.

The weight of the snow had bent a few young saplings across the path, creating obstacles we had to walk around. Dolton grabbed the end of a sapling and gave the branches a hard shake. Slowly the tree began to unbend and return to its upright form. The snow was soft and light, giving way beneath my snowshoe with a hush, a sigh of air released. Periodically I stopped and waited for Delores while Dolton hid beneath the spreading arms of an old spruce. The woods were nearly silent; few birds called; the wind was still. I could hear my breathing slow, become even after the trudge up the hill.

Past the first mile, beyond a tree farm sign that was tucked into a small clearing, down a long hall of nearly impassable branches bent across our path, we found the cedar trees. Tall, old, gnarled bark, with brown tips on many of the leaves, a sign of dry summers or a strong January thaw, the trees stood apart from the road. Grown beyond the reach of hungry deer, these cedar trees are among the few left in this area. "This is another symptom of colonized land," Delores said. "Deer didn't always live this far north. There used to be caribou and moose, and they didn't eat cedar trees."

We offered tobacco and a prayer and began to lop a few of the lower branches. Dolton insisted on holding the lopper but quickly lost interest. Somehow he climbed halfway up this thirty-foot tree while wearing snow-shoes. His voice echoed across the field, his new game of pretending to be stuck requiring a loud declaration to the world that he would not make it back. We tucked the last small branches into our carrying bags, told Dolton good-bye, that he was now a child to be raised by cedar, and made our slow, halting way back to the road.

He caught up with us before we had taken many steps. Again, just as he had done on the way down, he cleared a path for his grandmother by holding back branches that were lying across the road. Some he cut with the lopper and tossed to the side. He took the carrying bag from Delores and wore it down his back, the handle looped around his neck. When the path was unblocked, when we were again simply moving steadily uphill, he ran on ahead. Climbing the hill with ease, he called out, "I see the car!" His disembodied voice echoed through the trees as he disappeared beyond view. By the time we joined him, his snowshoes were packed in the trunk, his carrying bag placed in the back seat, and he was busy unwrapping Delores's mints, having hollered for permission first.

Back at their house, snug and warm with radiant heat that encouraged bare feet even in the dead of winter, Dolton made his long-promised hot chocolate for each of us. Still wearing his pajamas, even under his snow pants, he added a plush green robe for warmth. He bustled around the kitchen, heating water, carefully stirring each cup, and then plopping a mountain of whipped cream on top. The secret ingredient that raised this cup of chocolate to perfection was a piece of candy cane that added a subtle hint of mint. It was, as I told Dolton, the best cup of hot chocolate I had ever had.

We sat together in the living room, the same room where Dolton arrived when he was three years old, a small child in a state of panic, tormented by nightmares and unable to listen to or engage with anyone. Drawing from her lifetime of training, Delores knew she needed to allow Dolton to find his own way to share his experience. She lay down on the rug with him and said, "You tell Grandma your story. I'll sit and listen."

Over the next few months, without words, he acted out all the distress in his heart. He relaxed only when he was outside with Delores. She wrapped him in wool blankets and pulled him on a sled until he fell sound asleep.

When he grew older, he drew pictures and used words to share the memories that continued to surface. Some days when he refused to participate in anything, Delores would improvise a song she learned from her dad that would often pull him into an activity like setting the table. Sometimes he would break things, hit whatever was within reach, scream at the top of his lungs. Then Delores would wrap her arms around him and say, "Grandma is going to hold you until you're calm." Years later, he would pick up his unruly kitten and tell her, "I'm going to hold you until you're calm."

During the years that Delores was coordinating with a social worker to gain custody, Dolton would visit periodically, often dropped off by his mother for several months. Each time he left, Delores worried that he might not return. She knew, just as her grandfather knew, that he would need "concrete evidence that he was being listened to, he was being witnessed, he was surrounded with pure loving regard and unconditional acceptance of who he is." This would help him navigate whatever challenges he might face in his young life.

She chattered to him on one of their walks, striving to communicate these concepts in language that would reach a four-year-old. Dolton shouted, "Sing it, Grandma!" Delores sang,

In the evening when we're walkin'
tellin' the trees our story,
how our day went, what we're seeing, how we're feeling
we say "trees, you're our friends"
"trees, you're our friends"
then the trees say that they know us, they see us,
they hear us
they say "we hold you in our hearts"
"we hold you in our hearts"
they say "from the moment of your first breath, your first sight,
your first sound, your first gesture
we witness you, we know you
now you're crawlin,' now you're walkin,' you're running
you're leaping, joyous, innocent"
"we know you"
"we hold you in our hearts, we hold you in our hearts"
"we love you"

As they continue to build a life together around the tender love expressed in this song, Delores and Dolton share a mutual commitment to the beauty that is both within us and inherent in Native culture. Delores said, "Our commitment is to the beauty; beauty helps us find our way through the heartbreak."

"The healing spirits of the water gives life to our sacred Mother Earth and to all she nourishes."

—ALAMEDA ROCHA

Alameda Rocha

Alameda Rocha is a retired grandmother living in St. Paul who is committed to helping Dakota people become reconnected to their culture. The youngest of a large family, Alameda is enrolled on the Fort Peck Reservation, Montana, where she grew up. Fort Peck is home to the Dakota and Nakota, now known as the Fort Peck Tribes. Alameda spent three years at the Wahpeton Indian School between 1965 and 1968 after being removed from her home when she was twelve years old. Alameda shared her story:

"The memory of growing up at home, when I look at it today, it should never have been taken for granted. They were such beautiful people, and such beautiful things that we did as a community. People watched out for their children, helped one another out. Even if people were poor, we came together and were good to one another. There was always a gathering, like the 'celebrations,' our name for powwows. People spoke the language at home.

"Sometimes people would come and ask my dad to make a song. He would pray all night and by morning he had a song. He would try it out on us kids and teach it to us. If we were going to ceremony, my mother would tell me, *You have to sit still, no running around. The canupa is sacred. We come to learn something very beautiful.* I thought everybody was like that.

"My father passed away when I was nine. My mom went through a hard time. I remember standing in line for coal. Because of what the reservation went through in the 1950s and '60s, the government came through and said *we have to take these kids.* They took over four hundred children away. They had rules, white-society ways of thinking that they imposed on us. People hid their children. I was told never to answer the door if a white person was there.

"When they came through, my mom was crying. I climbed out the window and got away. Later on they came to school and took me. I didn't get to go home. They told me years later that my mother wasn't 'competent' because she couldn't type. I didn't understand that. We had a clean house, good food, and lots of love. They gave me the choice of boarding school or reform school or foster home. I went to the Wahpeton Indian School. The older kids had already gone to Pierre or Flandreau boarding schools.

"If it hadn't been for prayer morning and night, I would be in a mental institution. They told me, *Your family doesn't want you; your mother doesn't want you.* They took our sweet grass and sage. Said we couldn't speak Indian. We would go way out in the field to smudge and pray.

"I was careful about what I said. I couldn't trust people. Everyone was always getting demerits. They had to do hard labor to work them off. I remember a friend, someone died in her family and they wouldn't let her go home. I was getting fed up with them. How come I can't call home? They would open our mail first, wouldn't give it to us. If a family sent money or a package, we never got it.

"I told the girls, *I'm not staying anymore. Nobody cares. I'm leaving.* Girls were grabbing coats, hollering they were coming, too. There were maybe two or three from my reservation. We took off, but everyone was scared and crying. I couldn't take them all with me. We went back to our dorm. Somebody had already called the head matron. She cut our hair, *chop, chop,* chopped it off. She had a custom-made leather strap and beat us black and blue.

"She gave me an awful, hateful look in the mirror and raised the strap like she had pleasure in doing it, like I was something really bad. I didn't cry. She grabbed my hair and threw me in the shower. She dragged me out and threw me at the sink. She kept hitting me, calling me names, filthy Indian, heathen. I thought, *This woman is crazy. No one has ever hit me like this.* They took our clothes, gave us these old brown plaid dresses to wear. We had to get up early and do chores. I had to wear a sweater to cover the bruises on my arms. I was the so-called ringleader, so they had me kneel in the hallway all night on a broomstick. One of the hallway matrons from Sisseton gave me a blanket and pillow. She brought me chocolate milk and graham crackers. I was so thankful because I was so hungry. I didn't understand what I had done wrong.

"I remember this girl from Nebraska had a big thick braid that was cut off. When her mom came, she asked for the matron. *Are you the one who cut my daughter's hair?* Then the woman punched her. *I'm taking my daughter right now,* she said.

"I always prayed. I asked the Creator to forgive these people. After I had been there a while, I learned what they were about. Doing everything to convert everyone from being a savage. Asked me what religion I belonged to. I said Indian. *Where is that?* Everywhere. *When is it?* Every day. I thought that's how it's supposed to be. They said I had a split personality. They sent me to all these churches. I would either fall asleep or sneak out and sit outside. I didn't know what all these people were talking about. They were telling me when you come to church, you ask for forgiveness for your sins. What did I do wrong? I didn't understand. I fell asleep one time when the guy hits his pulpit. *The devil is in here!* Holy cripe! I looked around. There's no 'devil' in our religion. Who is that? How come the white people let him in their church?

"After I had stayed there three years, they wanted me to stay through the summer. Or I could do a six-week program at Flandreau. I heard Flandreau was nicer to Indians. When I got out of Flandreau, they sent me home. My mom didn't even know I was coming. She gave me a hug. *My girl, when did you get here?* She cooked and we visited.

"Next day we went to Grandpa's, where they talked Dakota. We went to town, picked up material, blankets, food. They had a ceremony for me. What happens to a person when they're severely abused, there were times when I didn't know if I was going to live or die. The elders were there at the ceremony, a few other people. They had me stand and smudge while they prayed. They told me I had a very strong spirit. I may not have known it, but the Creator was watching over me. When you believe in the Creator, you give it to him, and he takes care of it. I felt better. At Sundance, I always pray for those who didn't survive. A girl hung herself in the old building. How come she did that? She was pregnant. I was told a male matron did that to her. One committed suicide, she was beat up so bad.

"When my brothers came back from Pierre, they went into themselves. They wouldn't tell nobody what happened. One time I asked my youngest brother, Why do you drink? *For the pain,* he said. So go to a doctor; they'll give you medicine to quit drinking. *Nah, I'll be all right.* He sat there a while like he was debating if he should say more. He looked off in the distance. He said, *They took us downstairs in the basement when we were little. I was seven or eight years old. I remember my older brother told them,* Don't do that to my brother. Take me instead. *I was spared that time. They took me down later.*

"He started to cry. He said, *When I came back, I didn't feel like a man. I tried to have a relationship, but I couldn't. I have never had an honest relationship. I drank to cover it up.*

"I'm so sorry, I said. I'm so sorry."

All three of Alameda's brothers who attended boarding school died in alcohol-related accidents.

Alameda pointed to a stack of boxes in her apartment and said she wanted to take donated clothing back to her reservation in Montana. An elder had asked her to help their people. I nodded my head and assumed that we would have plenty of room in my car once everything was repacked into bags. I was not prepared, however, for the mountain of black plastic garbage bags waiting on the sidewalk when I pulled up, my car already laden with camping gear, a cooler, my own suitcase. At least a dozen bags filled to bursting were stacked on top of boxes of shoes, toys, a walker, and dolls. I thought we might have room for half of what she had managed to haul downstairs, her cane tucked in one corner of a grocery cart piled higher than her head.

"Alameda," I began, gesturing toward the bags.

"It will fit," she replied.

I started loading the bags into my Toyota, jamming every corner with something, approaching the task as if I were assembling a giant puzzle. The afternoon was hot and sultry, the humidity almost palpable in the air. As I worked, I could feel my t-shirt grow limp.

"I can help," a voice said behind me. One of the employees in Alameda's building stood looking at the car with a critical eye, judging the amount of space available against the large stack of goods that remained to be packed. "I used to work with a moving company." Ray proceeded to jam bag upon bag upon bag, poking small holes in the plastic to release air that was taking up precious cargo space. When he had reduced the pile to four bags, the car appeared to be completely filled.

"We did good," I said, thinking that the rest of the bags would simply have to wait for another trip.

"They'll fit," Ray replied, already pressing one of the bags into the mass, finally using his head to ram it into a crevice. Never mind that we would need to retrieve our luggage at some point, or that I had that morning baked a turkey for sandwiches which were now far beyond reach. Two more bags somehow vanished into the interior, and then the last bag appeared in Ray's hands. He jammed it in the side and then quickly pulled out his hand as he slammed the door. I understood that we could not expect to open any doors except the front until we reached our destination in Montana, twelve hours distant. I would have to drive using only side mirrors.

We shook hands with Ray, thanking him profusely for his efforts. As I pulled away from the curb, I could feel the difference the weight made in the way my car handled, the slight sway in the suspension. I did not realize that clothing could be so heavy.

When we stopped for the night in a small town between Fargo and Bismarck, North Dakota, I discovered it was possible to retrieve our luggage. The car was packed so tightly that I could pull each suitcase out and the surrounding bags remained wedged in place.

In the morning, we set sail on the low hills of the freeway, guarding my blind side by hugging the right lane of the road. The sky was a spotless blue, the sun already warming the mass of black plastic we carried. We passed the World's Largest Cow standing on a lonely hillside in the distance, followed by the World's Largest Buffalo. As we approached Medora on the western side of the state, the rolling hills grew sharp and fell away into valleys with hard edges forming buttes and ridges. The familiar, eerie landscape of the Badlands emerged on either side of the freeway.

We stopped at the roadside rest area to stretch our legs and admire the view. I stayed at Alameda's side as she walked slowly with her cane toward the fence. A young man stood on the opposite side with his toddler and dog, taking pictures, oblivious to the potential for rattlesnakes hiding among the warm rocks. Travelers stood near us taking pictures with their phones, reducing this vast, millions-years-old canyon to a two-inch-square image.

"Our ancestors would have known how to travel through this area," Alameda remarked, watching two hapless hikers below us hop from rock to rock, with no water bottles visible anywhere.

Looking at the buttes carved by wind and rain across so many generations, it was possible to feel time collapse in this austere, forbidding landscape. These otherworldly forms had evolved through slowly cascading rock, with layers stripped away by the wind across thousands of years. We were standing in front of a canyon that had been left mostly untouched by human intervention, a land not unlike what our ancestors had known.

As I mused, leaning on the top of the fence, I saw a tiny flick of motion far in the distance. My eye refocused on a small dark object on a plateau of sand-colored rock. It moved again. This time I could distinguish the motion of a tail swishing from side to side, a white face turned toward us. I was watching a wild mustang, part of a vanishing breed of horses that had never been tamed. I could see the hikers clattering toward the horse, still a good distance away. The mustang's head turned sharply toward the sound of the approaching hikers, its tail still moving with restless energy. Abruptly it wheeled about and ran deeper into the crevice between two buttes.

As we drove, Alameda would sometimes entertain me with stories, breaking into her infectious laugh, the wind carrying our voices out across the North Dakota hills. Then she would turn quiet, studying the view out her window as the miles carried us closer to her home. I could feel her distraction, her rising excitement at coming back to the land where she grew up, where she would soon be with her family at the Sundance. Then she would turn to me and speak seriously about protocol, what to expect, her own experience as a Sundancer. I listened carefully, absorbing her words while the warm wind whipped hair into my eyes, already feeling the heat of the sun overhead. I was both anxious—my first Sundance, my white face in a crowd of brown strangers—and relieved to be in the company of an experienced teacher, a woman who was sharing her knowledge with such generosity. For this trip, she would teach me the protocol and meaning behind the Sundance ceremony.

Although Alameda is enrolled at Fort Peck, she moved to Minnesota ten years earlier to be with her daughter. We met in 2002 at the first Dakota Commemorative March when she had followed an eagle to find the marchers on the road. My brother Dave and I had established an easy relationship with her right from the start. Alameda is willing to teach protocol to those of us who were not raised in our culture provided we ask in the right way. She said to me years later, "I felt the wound in some of the people on the March. I felt it in you."

We lost touch for five years or so when Alameda was absent from the subsequent Marches in 2004 and 2006. Then one day I was surprised to get a phone message from her, saying she had read my memoir, *Spirit Car,* and she remembered that we had met on the first March. Alameda told me about her daughter's kidney transplant, her own struggles with her health. She had done work for the Minnesota Historical Society, helping them to understand the meaning of ancient pictographs in southern Minnesota.

At a second meeting, Alameda suggested a trip back to Montana for the Sundance that was scheduled in mid-July. I listened but could not commit; I had just accepted a new job at the Dream of Wild Health farm that would begin a few weeks before the Sundance. We compromised: the trip would last only four days despite the fifteen hundred miles of driving it required.

Then Alameda raised the topic of the Mendota Mdewakanton tribe. She wanted to go to a tribal council meeting and invite them to the Sundance, where she was planning to offer prayers on their behalf. She had observed their struggles over the years to obtain federal recognition as a tribe, how they worked hard to recover their culture by teaching language tables and culture classes. Mendota, a French mispronunciation of the Dakota word *Bdote*, means the meeting of waters. Mendota is sacred to the Dakota as the creation site at the confluence of the Minnesota and Mississippi rivers.

At the tribal council, Alameda presented tobacco on the table and explained that its presence meant that she would be speaking truth. She explained who she was and how she had been observing Mendota's struggle for some time.

"This tribe is the most pitiful," she said, referring to their humble state, lacking a land base and federal recognition. Heads nodded around the table, acknowledging the truth of her words. She spoke of her reservation in Montana, how the Dakota people in Fort Peck had left Minnesota after 1851, eventually settling in the northeastern corner of the state. She referred to Minnesota as her original homeland.

"I am inviting all of you to come for Sundance," she said, naming a date two weeks distant. "I will be offering colors on behalf of Mendota."

Two weeks later, we were flying through the hills of eastern Montana, my car swaying gently with its burden. With all the black plastic pressed hard against the glass, it seemed as if we had tinted windows like those of the big SUVs that flew past us. Minnesota's cornfields and green pastures had long since given way to sun-baked hills and rough shallow-rooted shrubs that would dry into tumbleweeds in the fall. A few stunted trees grew in ravines except near the Missouri River, where a wide belt of deep green followed the water. Cattle grazed on stubby grass or lay in scarce shade to escape the afternoon sun. Irrigated fields of emerald-green alfalfa grew in checkerboard with acres of wheat, slowly turning a brilliant gold. The horizon had become infinite, even with the steeper terrain now carved into hills. At the top of each rise, we could see a storm approaching from the west while the south remained clear and bright.

We drove into Alameda's hometown, Wolf Point, in late afternoon and delivered our goods to a newly formed thrift store. Across the vast cavern of this metal warehouse, two volunteers were sifting through stacks of clothes, toys, books, and household items, moving slowly in the heat of the afternoon. When they first opened, they put an ad on the radio saying they were giving away free clothes. The next morning they had over three hundred people show up. When Alameda heard that they needed clothing and household items, she had immediately begun collecting donated goods and arranging this trip to deliver them.

After one more stop to deliver a bag of wild rice to an Ojibwe elder who was living far from his homeland in the Midwest, we headed toward the Sundance camp. Alameda had been told to watch for a double-wide trailer on the west side of the road. Just ahead of us, a fast-moving bank of dark clouds carried a wall of rain across dry fields, while behind us the sun was hot and bright. A long streak of lighting descended from clouds to ground, flashing near the turn for the Sundance. In our fascination with the storm's progress, we shot past the driveway and drove another five miles down the road toward the storm. A rainbow of intense hues made a graceful arc that seemed to end, as it always did, just beyond the next hill. As we rose to the crest of a tall slope, the end of the rainbow could be clearly seen in the valley below, a farmhouse and barn visible behind the shimmering bands of color.

We turned back, still dazzled by this image, and found the turn we had missed. Three slow-moving dogs approached the car as we honked and waited for someone to appear from the house. No one was home. We followed the twin dirt tracks that led toward the open fields, and a pickup appeared heading the opposite direction. A man stepped out of the truck and shook hands with Alameda. They spoke for a moment, renewing their acquaintance, before he gave us directions to the Sundance camp. When he said, "Turn by *the* shrub," I felt a new appreciation for the Minnesota woodlands we had left behind.

After a mile of following this deeply rutted track, we could see the tipis and tents of the camp set up on a plateau, the surrounding fields turning a mellow gold in the fading light of the setting sun. We had arrived in time to share a bowl of soup and to set up our tent in the near-dark, helped by three teenagers who simply jumped in and began setting stakes. "We're all family," Alameda said. That night we sat outside in lawn chairs and watched the stars emerge, their bright points filling the endless Montana sky.

For the next two days, I followed Alameda closely. I stood when she stood; I danced when she danced; I would have rested had she chosen to take any breaks. But a Sundance is about endurance and commitment and sacrifice and demonstrating a deep love for community so that the people will continue to live. I made mistakes, like staring intently at a Dakota man while he spoke, forgetting the cultural dictate of not making direct eye contact. This was my challenge, to remain rooted in one culture, to be mindful of what I was learning until it was so internalized that practice would become both habitual and instinctive. This is a deep, and difficult, lesson in humility. I am the equivalent of a gray-haired, middle-aged child, a beginner at an age when I should have been preparing to assume the role of elder.

During the breaks, we visited with Alameda's many relatives. We sat in the shade with a grandpa and his contented three-year-old grandson. The man smiled at the child and asked him, "How are you, grandson?"

The little boy looked up at him and replied, "I'm so happy." We all laughed, understanding exactly what he meant.

On the last morning, we sat at a picnic table in the area that had been set up for cooking and eating. Already the preparations were well under way for a magnificent feast to break the dancers' fast later that afternoon. A huge roaster had been wheeled behind the cooking shed and was now filled with large slabs of beef and buffalo that sizzled as they cooked. The mouthwatering aroma of barbecued meat filled the air each time the lid was lifted.

Later that morning, I sat next to a wiry, restless woman who was sometimes a bit querulous with her two female companions. I made small talk, searching for a common bond that would carry a conversation beyond our morning greeting. I asked, "Do you have children?"

"No."

"Any pets?"

"No."

I told her that I had a daughter and three stepchildren, including a fifteen-year-old teenager. For some reason, I mentioned that he struggled in school with a learning disability that made it hard for him to read. As I spoke, she listened intently, as if I was finally saying something that mattered.

She told me that she could not read or write either: "People don't know how difficult and humbling that is. You want to be equal with people, but it's such a struggle applying for jobs. I know I can do the work, but I can't fill out the papers. I have to humble myself to explain my situation. It keeps me close to spirit, that's what humility does.

"I had been gathering other plants one day and seen one I didn't recognize. Then my adopted brother, he talked about this plant. I said, *I think I know where it is*. It was that plant I seen. My nephew helped me dig it up, but I couldn't tell him what it was. The root was this big," she said, spreading her arms to measure a distance of about three or four feet.

"I made the medicine. It was a struggle because I'm a Christian, but I offered him a cup every day. The medicine gave him back his appetite. He was skinny from his cancer treatment, and he stopped eating. He got better, and he went to powwow. But my real faith is Christianity. That's 24/7 for me, not like Sundance where you go once a year and nothing happens in between."

The day before, she had set up her chair in the shade of the arbor, next to her two companions. Several times she had jumped up and walked around in the field that surrounded the arbor. Then she would return and sit with us again. She seemed nervous, unable to settle. Yet she was also part of the long line of supporters who followed the men around the circle.

The stress she was feeling was plain in her voice. I wondered if she felt torn between two paths to faith, if she had been led to believe that the presence of one denied the possibility of the other. Yet it seemed that this woman's gifts were so strong that she couldn't help but walk in both worlds. She was there participating yet struggling, as if pulled between two vastly different approaches to spirituality, not yet seeing their shared belief in the Creator. Unlike Clifford Canku, she had not yet found a peaceful way to combine both perspectives in her heart.

The first drumbeats could be heard from the arbor, the signal that the ceremony was about to begin. I was wearing the cotton print skirt I had made from a dress that Alameda had worn as a Sundancer years earlier, a gift she gave me before we left. She had shown me how to wrap my shawl around my waist. Alameda had changed to a new dress, one of several she owned from her years as a Sundancer. I had seen the stack on her closet shelf, carefully folded in a neat pile. When she selected one to give me, I knew that this was a special gift.

Alameda insisted that we place our chairs in the sun rather than find any comfort in shade. We left between "doors" to find water or to visit with some of Alameda's family or acquaintances. At the first sound of the drum, we returned to our chairs, although most of the time we danced in place, supporting the dancers inside the circle. I had never seen Alameda walk without leaning heavily on her cane. Yet she danced like a young woman, leaving her cane behind, keeping up with dancers who were decades younger.

Alameda's relatives, Leland Spotted Bird's family, had hosted this Sundance for many years. She grew up singing her father's songs with her siblings as they played powwow in the front yard. She said she thought everyone grew up with ceremonies. Then she came to Minnesota, where so often the story was one of loss from people who felt ashamed of not knowing their cultural traditions and their language. By relearning our history through events like the Dakota Commemorative March, I understood how this sense of loss and shame was part of the legacy of removal from the state.

Months earlier, Alameda had told me about her family and growing up at Fort Peck. When she talked about boarding school, she said, "I stayed strong because I was raised in ceremony. I could go to that place inside myself." Her mother went to Pierre Indian School, and her father attended the Carlisle Indian Industrial School.

Alameda's relatives belonged to two bands—Medicine Bear and Bad Temper Bear—that left Minnesota before the 1862 Dakota War. They moved west to the area that would become the Fort Peck Reservation. Alameda was born in Devils Lake (now Spirit Lake) and grew up in Wolf Point. In 1969, she married an Ojibwe man and moved to the Red Lake Reservation in Minnesota, where they raised two children. Alameda returned to Montana after they divorced in 1975. When she struggled with anger and bitterness, she turned again to the elders for support. They took her through ceremony and told her, "When you believe in the Creator, then you give it to him and he takes care of it." Throughout the difficult times in her life, Alameda has relied on her faith, her ceremonial life, and the guidance of spiritual leaders who cared for her and her family. In 1997, they told her it was time to return to Minnesota.

After being led by an eagle to participate in the 2002 Dakota March, Alameda had to turn her attention to her family. She helped her youngest daughter—who was diagnosed with type 1 diabetes when she was twelve— through a kidney transplant. Her son had been killed in a car accident when he was just twenty-one years old, and her oldest daughter passed away from lupus, leaving behind six children and a grandchild. "Love your children and your grandchildren like it was the last day of your life," Alameda said. "Our children are a gift from the Creator."

While living far from home, Alameda stayed in close touch with her relatives and spiritual leaders. Through her travels to ceremonies and pow-wows, she met Naida Medicine Crow, a young woman from the Crow Creek Reservation who had grown up in the foster care system. As they came to rely on each other, Naida would eventually become like a daughter to Alameda.

One Sunday afternoon, we picked up Naida at the Catholic Charities in Minneapolis, where she works most weekends helping chronic alcoholic men. She had only an hour, she said, before her teenage daughter came home. We decided on a quick stop at Perkins.

Standing next to Alameda and Naida, I felt like a giant. Naida is short but strongly built, with thick dark hair pulled back from her face. Her eyes are careful, observant. Alameda insists that she is a hint taller. She too wears her long hair in a bun, streaks of gray framing her round face, her brown eyes shining behind hip glasses. Naida's phone rang frequently with calls from her daughter.

As Naida told her story, it was hard to imagine her as the lonely, angry child she once was. At thirty-five, Naida is an articulate, poised young woman who has grown up to become a conscientious mother, despite having few role models in her early life. Her parents were both teenagers from Crow Creek. Her mother moved with Naida to Minneapolis without telling Naida's father. When Naida was five, social services removed her from her home, citing her mother's drinking as the reason for terminating her parental rights. Despite the passage of the Indian Child Welfare Act three years earlier in 1978, they failed to contact either the tribe or Naida's family in Crow Creek, where she was enrolled, and instead placed her in white foster care.

For the next ten years, Naida believed that she had no family. She felt completely alone and unloved, disconnected from her culture, and deeply angry. She was shuffled through a series of white foster homes where she suffered emotional and physical abuse and was shamed for being Native.

After years of running away and acting out her rage, Naida made friends with a family at Prairie Island who introduced her to ceremony. There was something that drove her not to give up, to deal with her anger and turn her life around. As she struggled to understand her Native identity, her friend advised her to find out about her family. When she was fifteen, Naida wrote to her aunt at Crow Creek, who said they had been waiting all these years for Naida to find them. Her dad had a picture of her as a baby on a star quilt that he still carried in his wallet. He never knew where Naida and her mother had disappeared to, nor did social services ever contact him or his family. In one visit to Crow Creek, Naida changed from having no family to being part of a large one.

While she was attending college in Mankato, Naida became pregnant with her daughter, Dakota. Her foster family advised her to give up the baby. Naida absolutely refused to put her child through that experience. She quit school and returned to Minneapolis, where she found work at a foster group home for Native boys aged fourteen to eighteen. She discovered she had a gift for helping others, such as these boys, find their way through the heartbreak and loneliness of foster care. While she still struggled with anger, Naida found a way to turn her experience into compassion and understanding for others.

"All of my experiences have made me into who I am," Naida said. "I'm in a place now where I can help people."

Years later, one of the young teens wrote and expressed his thanks. He said, "I love you because you accepted me for who I am." Naida treasures that letter, knowing that her experience helped her make a difference in someone's life. Currently she works as an employment counselor at the American Indian Opportunities Industrialization Center (AIOIC). Ultimately, her dream is to become a lawyer and advocate for Native people.

"I would like people to know that no matter what you go through, no matter what obstacles you face, you can make it," Naida said. "You can overcome anything. This was Creator's way that I was meant to go. I was ashamed of being taken away. People told me that I could do anything I wanted, so don't give up. There were certain people who were put in my path who helped me."

One of those people was Alameda, who was there to listen and offer encouragement as Naida struggled to put together the pieces of her life. Alameda explained that she was taught to pray and dance for the ones who are having hard times, for the children yet to come, and for those who were lost, just as our ancestors prayed for us. Part of colonization, she said, is not knowing that our ancestors prayed for us long before we were born, knowing that our children's children, our seven generations, are the future. "That must be how I made it," Naida said.

As they grew closer, sharing their stories and forming a strong bond over time, eventually they chose to adopt each other as family. In the Native way, this happens through a hunka ceremony, the making of relatives, where the relationship is acknowledged before the Creator. Hunka ceremonies help families who have lost a loved one or want to acknowledge a special relationship, as in the child-beloved ceremony.

"She is my child-beloved," Alameda said. "Naida will be recognized at the Sundance as my daughter. My children will become her sister; my relatives will be her relatives." Through her commitment, Alameda accepts responsibility to guide and mentor Naida throughout her life, just as a mother would guide her daughter. In turn, Naida, who has never known this relationship with her own mother, has made a relative in a traditional way who will help heal that absence in her life.

I cannot imagine a more touching image: the wounds of boarding school and foster child bound by the loving embrace of an ancient tradition.

A year after our trip to the Sundance, Alameda and I made another quick four-day visit to Montana to talk with some of her relatives who had agreed to share their understanding of raising beloved children in a traditional way. After accepting tobacco from me to be part of this work, Alameda had taken an active role in suggesting people to interview, checking on my progress, nudging me to find a time to go to Montana. Finally, in early June, we left St. Paul before dawn. I had packed a new digital recorder for the interviews, extra batteries for my camera. This was my writing armor, the tools I carry with me when I go to gather stories from strangers.

On this trip, however, my tools would never even leave the bag. I was arriving in Montana with a mind trained by white schools and imprinted by English. I had yet to see how that training determines how we interpret the world: Native history defined through the lens of the invaders; Native languages displaced by English, a trade language; learning through experience replaced with books and rote memorization; oral tradition replaced by notebooks and recorders. If a Native person also gives up involvement in ceremony, stops going to powwows, then there is little defense left against the way of life taught in school. My brief time in Montana was an unconscious continuation of the process to "unschool" my heart and mind, in the phrase I learned from Harley and Sue Eagle.

On this trip, we would spend most of our time in Wolf Point, a small town of about three thousand residents. Established in 1879 as a sub-agency and trading post for the Fort Peck Reservation, the town is pre-dominantly white, unlike nearby Poplar, which serves as the headquarters for the reservation. Fort Peck is home to two nations: the Dakota and the Nakota. Prior to and following the 1862 Dakota War, Dakota exiles from Minnesota fled to Canada, North and South Dakota, and Montana. In recent years, an effort has been made to reconnect with this early his-tory and recognize Minnesota as the original homeland for many of the Dakota now living at Fort Peck.

Our first stop was to visit Caleb Shields, a retired chairman and council-man of the Fort Peck Reservation. We brought gifts: two pounds of short ribs, pilot bread or "Nakota fry bread," green tea, cloth. A riding lawn mower was parked on the sidewalk, a handful of tools spread nearby. Caleb greeted us at the door, a lean man with graying hair pulled back in a pony-tail, the cuffs of his shirt rolled neatly above his wrists. We sat at the kitchen table where his laptop was still running.

In his younger days, Caleb Shield was a "big dog" in the world of pub-lic policy and Native politics. He was given an honorary doctoral degree from the University of Montana–Missoula for his life experience, the highest honor they offer. In a publication that described his early years at the Pierre boarding school, the article ended with a glowing Congres-sional tribute to him written by Senator Max Baucus when Caleb retired in 1999.

"He has stood in the Halls of Congress, often in the face of severe oppo-sition, defending the governmental and sovereign rights of the tribes. He has stood up to the federal government when the federal government has failed in its obligation to the tribes of this country. Significantly, he did all this without ever making an enemy and without ever treating any person with disrespect. We can all stand to learn something from this man who while he had many battles, he never made any enemies."

When he visited Minnesota as part of the first "We Are One" conference organized by Alameda and Naida, Caleb spoke about the book he published with several other writers. Titled *The History of the Assiniboine and Sioux Tribes of the Fort Peck Indian Reservation, Montana, 1800–2000,* the book provides a detailed history of the tribes up to recent times, including the diaspora that brought many Dakota to Montana.

On the wall of Caleb's "fun room," near the bustle he wears while dancing, hang numerous awards. Caleb is prominent in photographs taken when he served as an advisor on Native affairs to many legislators, government officials, and even President Clinton. He was one of the few chairmen actually to retire from the position, after serving a remarkable twenty-four years, rather than being ousted in subsequent elections. As we stood near the door to say good-bye, he showed us pictures of his grandchildren, including his grandson in uniform who was serving in Iraq.

Meeting Caleb offered an inspiring role model of a Native person who was committed and active in ceremonial life yet equally committed and successful in pursuing public policy work as a way of improving life for Native people. Caleb had successfully navigated the rocky shoals of both legislative and tribal political spheres. Yet it was clear that his commitment to spiritual life was at the core of his life and work.

We visited others throughout the day, including Catherine Spotted Bird, a well-respected elder whose daughter served us homemade soup while she visited with Alameda. Instinctively, I understood that it was not appropriate to ask about recording our conversation or taking pictures. While her new grandchild slept near us in his infant seat, I asked about raising beloved children. Catherine thought for a moment before saying, "Children learn by example."

After a quick stop at a rummage sale, we visited one of the tribe's spiritual leaders, Larry, who at first seemed far too young for this role. Sitting with him on his patio drinking ice water, I was surprised to hear him talk of grandchildren at college. He too, like Caleb, radiates a strong physical presence, the vital energy of a man who is tested in Sundance, who maintains his life so that he is ready and capable of giving his best at any moment. His immediate response to my question about raising beloved children was to talk about returning to the old way of addressing each other by relationship rather than name. That way, young people grow up learning who their family members are, how they're related, and the appropriate way of behaving toward them—a practical step toward reinforcing cultural training.

Ella Deloria explains in *Speaking of Indians* that the Dakota words "to address a relative" and "to pray" are very similar. You can only be sure of your own relatives, who are bound by kinship rules not to harm each other, so it makes sense to establish immediately how people are related to each other. Otherwise, strangers might turn out to be an incarnation of Iktomi, who was always looking to play tricks on those who are not careful. Using the proper kinship term obligates the speaker to assume the right mental attitude and correct behavior toward the person being addressed. Ultimately, this exacting obedience to kinship demands made the Dakota a kind and unselfish people.

Larry told a story about how important it is to remain positive even when we're struggling. He was asked to tutor his granddaughter, Justice, who was having a hard time understanding math. He told her, "Every morning when you get up, stand in front of the mirror and say three times, *Justice is very good at math.* Do this for a month. If nothing changes, then you will be allowed to quit summer school." Her grades improved immediately, and she went on to college, where she excelled in math.

Our visit with Leland Spotted Bird was the last stop before getting back on the road toward home. We had to wait until late in the afternoon because he needed to prepare for ceremony. When we drove up, he was in the front yard helping his son fix his car. Several friendly dogs wandered up, hoping for a handout. Farther up the hill, near the tracks that led to the Sundance grounds, two shiny toy windmills sparkled in the sun.

We were introduced to two teenage grandsons. When the older boy was three years old, he had shown up at the front door with his suitcase. Leland asked him, "Are you going to stay with Grandpa for awhile?" He said yes. He was still there at nineteen, learning traditional teachings directly from Leland.

Inside, Leland's wife, Doris, was sitting in an upholstered rocking chair while Leland perched on a stool near her. Occasionally the grandsons would wander through. The younger one brought a chair and sat in the middle of our small group, eating thick wedges of sausage and bread. A daughter came in carrying a two-year-old also known as "the Boss," who cast stern eyes at Alameda and me if we seemed too friendly with her grandpa. Doris said, "We like to spoil a grandchild up to a certain age."

On the weekends, their house is often filled with grandkids and their friends. Some come for ceremony; others come for the first time because they are curious. Many of them return wanting to learn more. Teenagers are instinctively drawn to the places where their needs are met—for acceptance, for role models, for learning about life in a way that is relevant to their personal development. Here, they spend time on the land at a home where little importance is placed on material things. They are welcomed, fed, and taught about ceremony and Native values in ways that nurture their spirits. Leland and Larry both referred to an identity crisis in Native kids, some of whom dress and behave in the gangster style like African American or Latino youth, wearing baggy trousers and talking tough. "After they start coming to ceremony," Leland said, "that changes. As they learn their own culture, they gain a sense of belonging."

In everything they do, Leland and Doris keep an eye on the future, knowing that at this stage of their lives, their role is to teach kids to assume responsibility for maintaining traditions. They need to grow up knowing and feeling the love that is central to Native culture and experiencing their connection to the spiritual world as a birthright, one to be respected and nurtured.

After sitting with us for awhile, Doris went into the kitchen. I heard her say to no one in particular, "I'll fix something to eat." Periodically she would come back into the room and stand behind her chair, her hands covered in flour. Later she would offer homemade soup and gabooboo bread, giant wheels of perfect fry bread.

Although he has since retired, Leland at that time was still employed as a prosecutor for the tribe. In his work in law enforcement, he has seen the devastating impact alcohol has had on Native people. Fortunately, Leland did not grow up with alcohol in his family. His grandmother never spoke English, so he learned to speak Dakota by spending time with her. When he asked to go to boarding school, his mother refused to sign the paper because she didn't want him to have the same experience she had.

Throughout his life, Leland has encouraged his children and grand-children to have a strong commitment to ceremony and spiritual practice. His pride was obvious as he told how their kids and grandkids all Sun-dance or powwow dance, sing, and participate in sweat lodge. There is a computer in a corner of the room with a large file of songs on it. Some-times the grandsons will go online and Google the names of the warriors they hear about in ceremony, exploring their history in a unique blend of contemporary and traditional learning.

"What is most important," Leland said, "is prayer and making a com-mitment to your spiritual life. When you pray, when you ask the Creator for help. What makes a difference is your level of commitment, what you are willing to offer in return. Pray from the heart, not the head. There's a big difference. Everything is reciprocal. To ask of the Creator, you have to be willing to give back."

When I mentioned the genius and brilliance of Native culture, want-ing to portray something beyond the broken images and statistics in the media, Leland nodded his head. "Not everyone understands that about the culture," he said. "Understanding and seeing what is so powerful about our culture will help bring about healing."

But there are steps to follow, a progression of learning that has a begin-ning, middle, and advanced stage. Typically, a person is raised in his or her culture from infancy, absorbing language, behavior, and expectations like a tiny sponge so that the essence permeates into the skin, muscles, bones, unconscious thought, deep within the spirit. When this process is broken, as it was in boarding schools, it has to be learned consciously while still following the same stages of beginning, middle, and advanced. Leland said, "You begin as an infant and grow from that point." Some people try to leapfrog over stages, especially if they begin the learning process when they're older. People want to begin in the middle or later, quickly assuming the mantle of shaman to alleviate the insecurity of being a beginner as an older person. But this process is also a valuable teaching for the lesson of humility, one that is not encouraged in our broader society. As Joseph M. Marshall III pointed out, humility is "the one strength that gives true meaning to all the others."

"Learning the protocol is important," Leland said, "because you have to know how to conduct prayers and ceremony correctly or consequences will follow." That's one reason Leland spends so much time helping young people learn—there's a great need for leadership coming from the next generation.

I could see why kids are drawn to Leland and Doris. They share the same gentle fierceness, the same balance of strength and kindness that I felt in my mother. Never an angry word toward children, and yet children know instinctively what is expected from them. In Leland there is a deep thoughtfulness, a self-awareness that arises from time spent in prayer and in ceremony, and self-confidence that comes from humility and not ego. He shares the same sense of physical power and strength that I recognized in Caleb, Larry, and Clifford Canku. All are contemporary warriors, combining physical strength regardless of age and integrity with a deep spiritual commitment. As parents and grandparents, Leland and Doris exemplify the words of his sister, Catherine Spotted Bird, in providing role models for children to learn from. In their daily lives, they demonstrate the values of the culture: sober, disciplined, generous, kind, humble. Proud.

Finally, Leland said to me, gently, that it is very difficult to speak conceptually about what he does because "it's a way of life." Other people have come and asked questions as I have, including a film crew who showed up and wanted him to explain everything on film. We don't see how our thoughts, our actions, our way of learning have been defined by the language we are taught, by the history we learn, and the way that the physical world has been drained of its life and set down on paper. We are taught to learn through reading and writing, conceptualizing experience and developing the aspect of the mind that deals with abstract thought. We come unprepared to understand that this way of life, this culture, this process of learning is based on experience. "You can't read it in a book," Leland said.

"Then what I will write," I replied to Leland, "is that it's a way of life." Through the process of writing this book, I have learned that I can go only to a certain point, right up to that statement. If I want to go further in my understanding, I need to commit personally to the ceremonies and allow them into my spirit, changing the person I am now. "But ceremonies are not something I can write about," I said, "so I'm in a bit of a quandary as a writer. I may have to switch to fiction." Both Leland and Alameda laughed. But I knew when he spoke that I had come to the end of the road. Unschooling, indeed.

Here's what I learned in this humble home where the furniture is well worn from years of raising children and grandchildren. If that's all you see, if you come with an eye that is trained only to see the surface of things, you'll miss the point: that inside this home are people who are living with the highest commitment to the values and teachings of the culture, who have made their spiritual lives and the well-being of their children and grandchildren the highest priority. Regardless of the material comfort in the lives of the people we had visited, it was clear that what was central to all of them, and of greatest importance in their community, was their disciplined commitment and devotion to ceremony, to their families, and to their people.

What I learned is that you have to live your life so that you're prepared to give your best efforts, your highest thoughts, your love and passion to your people. Your thoughts today are creating your future. Your actions create your strength; you maintain the body you will have as you age. This is not Sunday church living. This is a spirituality that demands the highest capability of each person, of living directly from that place of connection and communion, where spirituality is not a part-time effort or a mask for hypocritical acts. It literally means infusing every day with prayer, with a consciousness of the values that are central and fundamental to the culture, of acting in accordance with those values.

"Our grandpa taught us to pray for the ones coming behind us who are the future," Alameda said. "Whatever tools we have, we lay down a foundation for our children so they grow to be strong. We teach them our values, our spirituality, about the Creator, to be good to one another."

Statement by the Assistant Secretary of the Bureau of Indian Affairs

At the ceremony acknowledging the 175th anniversary of the establishment of the Bureau of Indian Affairs, September 8, 2000, the remarks of Kevin Gover, Assistant Secretary-Indian Affairs, Department of the Interior, included the following comments:

This agency forbade the speaking of Indian languages, prohibited the conduct of traditional religious activities, outlawed traditional government, and made Indian people ashamed of who they were. Worst of all, the Bureau of Indian Affairs committed these acts against the children entrusted to its boarding schools, brutalizing them emotionally, psychologically, physically, and spiritually. Even in this era of self-determination, when the Bureau of Indian Affairs is at long last serving as an advocate for Indian people in an atmosphere of mutual respect, the legacy of these misdeeds haunts us. The trauma of shame, fear and anger has passed from one generation to the next, and manifests itself in the rampant alcoholism, drug abuse, and domestic violence that plague Indian country. Many of our people live lives of unrelenting tragedy as Indian families suffer the ruin of lives by alcoholism, suicides made of shame and despair, and violent death at the hands of one another. So many of the maladies suffered today in Indian country result from the failures of this agency. Poverty, ignorance, and disease have been the product of this agency's work.

And so today I stand before you as the leader of an institution that in the past has committed acts so terrible that they infect, diminish, and destroy the lives of Indian people decades later, generations later. These things occurred despite the efforts of many good people with good hearts who sought to prevent them. These wrongs must be acknowledged if the healing is to begin.

Star Spirit

BY GABRIELLE TATEYUSKANSKAN

Beloved child you were brought to earth by the Wicanhpi Oyate
Falling to earth you were formed in the imagination of
the people through origin narrative
Spirit was manifest in the flesh of the living
Hopes of the ancestors flow in your blood
Your first breath
a soft soothing song
Singing the story of the lives that have come and gone
before you
Lives that paved the way for your coming
By a falling star you were entrusted to me
A sacred gift from the Creator
To care for
and
protect with my heart

A Silent Voice

If you ask us, "What is silence?" we will answer, "It is the Great Mystery. The holy silence is God's voice."

—OHIYESA (Charles Alexander Eastman)

A late March snowstorm has flung a blanket of snow and ice across the newly exposed fields at the Dream of Wild Health farm. Dark, moist soil has refrozen; migrating birds seek shelter in the foliage of spruce and pine trees. A week earlier, sandhill cranes had called their loud *kar-r-r-o-o-o* as they flew overhead, while the red-winged blackbird trilled from the wetland, and the robin chirped its joy at finding withered crabapples still hanging from the trees. Behind the house, a woman fanned the smoking embers of damp wood, patiently encouraging a fire to catch hold. The fire is for the women who came to honor the equinox as spring returned with her uncertain, volatile moods.

Inside the warm glow of the kitchen, a small group of Dakota and Ojibwe women has gathered for a retreat led by Ida Downwind. Much of the weekend will be spent in silence until the closing ceremony on Sunday. The women will eat and drink sparingly, focusing their attention on prayer.

We sit talking around the same table where I first met Delores five years earlier. Bright squares of red and yellow cloth are stacked near half-drunk cups of tea. There is a sense of anticipation and an undercurrent of anxiety about not speaking for two days, stepping out of comfortable routines and eating habits, far from the constant noise and activity of young children and the city.

Ida Downwind, an Ojibwe elder, spent many years in South Dakota taking part in Lakota ceremonies that helped her heal from years of physical abuse. Through her participation in fasting and Sundance, she was given permission to lead the *inipi,* or sweat lodge ceremony. We talked briefly about historical trauma, how it was evident throughout the Native community. When Ida spoke about the trauma in her life, she said in a matter-of-fact tone, "I have forgiven the unforgiveable."

She had asked for a retreat at the farm so that this circle of women could rest and spend time in prayer. By calling for silence and fasting, she relieved them of their social obligations and the deeply ingrained habit of caring for others by cooking, tending, chatting, parenting. They could not distract themselves by talking or by careless eating. They simply had to be.

When they came in late that night from the fire, their feet covered in dried mud and their spirits cleansed with prayer, when they fell exhausted into their beds, the silence that descended on the house was deeper than that of sleep, reaching far beyond dreams to the stars that filled the night sky.

The gift of this weekend, the gift of not speaking, came as they remembered how to listen to the Creator. The gift of silence allowed them to listen to their own hearts and to hear what the Creator is saying.

Many of us have forgotten how to do this. We're too busy; our children need our attention; jobs are demanding; there's never enough time. Sometimes we're so exhausted, we have to sleep, and sleep, and sleep. And then there's all the pain that surfaces when we first quiet our minds, when there is nothing to dull the grief that rises, or the rage that burns like a fire, or the loneliness that is the most frightening of all, the emptiness of dead space— the reasons why people keep their televisions turned on all the time.

If you can find your way back to the silence, if someone like Ida is there to help plant the seed, then this is the first step toward returning to a Dakota way of life, to once again raise beloved children. As Dakota historian David Larsen said, "If you know what was taken away, then you can reclaim it."

When Glenn Wasicuna said to me, years earlier, "Heal yourself first," I didn't know what he meant. I didn't know what healing was. It's easy to see the consequences of trauma, to read the mounting statistics of suicide, addiction, disease, and poverty as symptoms of the underlying harms that have been passed down through generations and inherited by our children. Far more difficult, I believed, was to find the way to resolve the problems. Just look at Canada's experience with reparations; that action triggered nearly two dozen suicides, simply from having residential school memories reawakened. That's when I started asking people in this book— Harley and Sue Eagle, Clifford Canku, Gabrielle Tateyuskanskan, Delores Brunelle, and Alameda Rocha—how they have confronted trauma and transformed the challenges they faced in their lives, redirecting their energy into positive efforts for themselves, their families, and their communities.

I heard and witnessed stories that touched me deeply. As I entered into their lives, I had to listen with my entire being in order to do justice, to do honor to the trust they placed in me. I felt each story grow into a being shared between us, a living spirit that might go out into the world for others to hear. The assumptions with which I began this work started to give way to new, deeper understanding. I thought that as Dakota people, we had a responsibility to learn our language so that it wouldn't disappear, that we needed to be part of the ceremonies because they teach our values, providing form to a spirituality that is not confined to a church. I was looking for big, broad teachings that would spark a faith I didn't know how to find.

Instead, each person showed me in small ways how to act, how to treat people, how to speak up, where to go when the work was hard. As they told me their stories, I learned how to listen. In sharing their vulnerable moments, they showed me humility. By collaborating in this work, they taught me about respect. Over the years that have passed since I first started this book, something began to relax, to slow down, to open. I learned to pray every day as a commitment to this process, believing that these stories were sacred, that my words had to come from spirit. Even my writing process shifted, becoming less focused on thinking and more concerned with the spiritual aspects of the work. "I'm just the typist," I would say. Strangely, when I tried to define what was shifting in me, I lacked words. I felt instead like weeping.

It was Glenn Wasicuna who explained that the Dakota word for prayer was *cekiya*, which means "to cry to God." Without words, from the heart.

"Long ago," Glenn told me, "Dakota people were given all they needed to create a way of life that was beautiful in its regard for all other beings." We were given language and a way to pray, we were given ceremonies to teach us how to keep our hearts open, and we were given seven traditions that define who we are as Dakota people. We were shown the way and given the ceremonies to help us try every day to live up to that vision.

As Clifford Canku explained, this is *WoDakota*, having the true traditions of the Dakota way of life. "Every day is a learning experience, unraveling what you're supposed to do, becoming Dakota every day."

"It's a sad, sad world for the Dakota," Glenn said. "We have replaced the recipe the Creator gave us with a lot of man-made thoughts." Glenn is a first language speaker and teacher from the Sioux Valley Reserve in Manitoba, Canada. We were sitting in a quiet room at Minnesota State University, Mankato, in the city where the thirty-eight Dakota warriors were hanged. I had come to ask his permission to tell the story of our first conversation years earlier. What he gave me was a deeper understanding of what his words meant.

When Glenn said, "Heal yourself first," he meant, *Learn what it means to be Dakota.* He said, "I want to share with you what makes up the Dakota Nation. There are seven traditions that we were originally given by the Creator. He gave us a recipe to live by. This recipe is so wonderful, so beautiful, yet we stray from it. We add things, we try to change it. Or we don't even use the recipe at all." Generations of trauma have displaced this original vision so that we now live out of balance, not even seeing what has been lost.

From his wallet, Glenn pulled out a well-worn piece of paper on which he had written seven words in Dakota.

All of these traits, or traditions, work together to hold a vision of who we are as the Dakota Nation, the Oyate. They work in order. You can't skip around or pass one up. Like steps, each one must be learned thoroughly before moving on. The strength we gain in understanding each tradition will help us meet the next one.

"The first tradition is so important," Glenn said, "that we will return to it after discussing the other six."

Dependability. As Glenn stated this second tradition, I thought to myself, I know this. A chronic workaholic like me can be counted on for anything. Glenn explained that to be dependable meant the burden is on you to take care of yourself first. You do what you have to do, including eating well, going to sweat lodge, and praying. The Creator said, don't ask me for honesty, or bravery, or strength. I gave you everything already. The only thing you can ask for is your health. You can pray for health to make yourself dependable to your family. If others see that you are dependable, then they will try harder to be dependable, too. They will become healthier, and the Nation will become stronger.

Respectfulness. This is a word that gets used a lot in conversation. I respect this person and that person, but that's not really what the Creator had in mind. What he meant is that you respect yourself because you were born sacred. The Dakota word for child means "like God." So God put you in this world in a sacred way. The way we move, the shape of our ears, our faces, our voices are all gifts of the Creator. To show respect, you take care of your self. When others see that you carry yourself in a respectful way, that you speak in a respectful way, then they will try harder to be respectful. The Nation will get stronger again.

Helpfulness. If you do the first steps, then you can help yourself. You do what you need to do to take care of yourself and your family. You become strong, honest, dependable, and respectful. Then others will also want to be like that. They'll say, "Look how she takes care of herself and her family and her home." The Nation becomes like that. Then if someone else needs help, you can go and help.

Compassion. You look at the gifts the Creator gave you, and you take care of them. You show compassion for yourself, understanding, and humility. Others will say, "This is such a beautiful sight, how she cares for herself in a compassionate way, how she is dependable, respectful, and helpful. I want to be like that." The Nation will become like that. People will talk well of themselves and others, too, because they have compassion.

Positiveness. A Dakota person is always thinking and talking in a positive way. Whenever you think about yourself and your things, be positive.

Choose well what you put into your body. Choose your words so that you speak well. When people know that positive words come from your mouth, they will listen to you. The Nation will become more like that.

Bravery. To hold together all of these traditions, bravery means that you can stand up with courage when others say, "Who does she think she is?" This means you can be brave for yourself because you already know that you are dependable, respectful, helpful, compassionate, and positive. You don't have to tell people off; you don't have to feel rage at not doing all these things as a Dakota person. The Nation becomes strong when the people carry within themselves the bravery they need to live according to these traditions.

After we discussed these six traits, Glenn asked if I knew what the first tradition must be. "Faith?" I asked.

"It's in there," he said.

"Love?"

"It's in there, too."

Finally, he told me:

Silence. The first tradition, together with bravery, is the most important in holding together this entire vision. Even though the world shows little respect for those who are quiet, believing that it's too easy for people to run right over you, to think you're slow or unwilling to defend yourself, silence teaches the most fundamental trait of being Dakota. Silence allows you to listen and to hear the voice of the Creator. You have to have Silence to hear what God is saying.

Following this path, or recipe, requires discipline and commitment. When Glenn was growing up, his dad told him, "It's hard to be an Indian." Glenn thought he meant it was hard because they were poor or because people didn't like Indians. His dad meant, *It's hard to follow the original recipe for Dakota people.*

What many of us have lost is the sacredness in the way we live. We have replaced Silence with jealousy and gossip, with living out of balance. We've set aside prayer as the first, essential step toward regaining not just a way of life, but a way of living. We haven't lost the language because people have stopped speaking it; we've lost the sacredness that invited language to be present. "When the Creator gave us the Dakota language," Glenn said, "he told us, *Don't speak from your mind; speak from your heart. I gave you this language so that you can talk to me.*" Prayer comes from the heart, from feelings that are the language of spirit. Glenn told me that Dakota people pray all the time.

"When the Creator put us on this earth," Glenn continued, "he gave each one of us something to do while we're here. When our time is up, we go. But the Creator is going to ask, *Did you do what I asked you to do?* How will we answer that question if we never take the time to listen? How will we recognize *what is ours to do*?"

I could begin to see how ceremonies help to instruct and support these seven traits. The sweat ceremony, for example, was given to Dakota people with specific instructions on how and why we use it, even the songs to sing. The *inipi* is a practical teaching about the Dakota way of silence, of praying and listening to the Creator. The pipe is the equivalent of the Bible. Since these traditions were not intended to be read in a book, ceremonies teach us who we are through our bodies and our spirits.

I think of all the times I've read lists of Dakota values, each time assuring myself that I was well on my way to learning each one. But I was not really getting the point until Glenn was willing to sit with me and explain it. Through his voice, his intonation, his questions, the feelings he expressed, through the many silences that punctuated our conversation, I made a connection with the teachings because they came through a relationship, because I knew him, because he cared that I understood his meaning. Yet here we are, surrounded by words, because a person must begin somewhere.

When faith or prayer or spirituality becomes once-a-week church living, whether it's Native spirituality or Christian or Islamic, when it ceases to be a primary guide for each day, then it's all too easy to become swept up by the distractions around us. The Rosebud Sioux website states, "A religion becomes a way of life when we choose to participate in it creatively, rather than witness it passively." If you're not mindful of the values at the core of your spirituality, it's easier to rationalize your own benefit at the expense of others. If that means putting a shopping mall where there used to be a wetland, or marketing fast food to impressionable kids, or breaking a treaty, what's the difference? Confess, and your sins are forgiven.

For Dakota people, we need to know that "our traditional values are sacred laws and spiritual laws that hold us accountable to a truth," explained Janice Bad Moccasin, Crow Creek, a Hunkpati Dakota Winyan who helps her people with spiritual assistance. "We want to develop our cultural identity. We want to develop a healthy spirituality based on traditional, sacred holy laws."

From that strong spiritual core flow all other forms of challenging injustice, all of the ways of working to improve the lives and health of Native people in this country and to protect the well-being of Mother Earth. As explained in the book *The Sacred Tree*, "From this position of strength, no one can put us down, and no one can lead us to do or to be anything else but what we know we must do or be."

The Sacred Tree, a collection of indigenous teachings created by the Four Worlds Development Project, a Native intertribal group, offers the lesson of balance through the medicine wheel. "Balance, when applied to the interconnectedness of all human beings, becomes justice . . . Without it, there can be no peace or security in the affairs of the world."

By living each day to the best of our abilities, we practice WoDakota, a commitment to the sacred laws and traditions that will help us use our individual gifts to rebuild a better world for our children. While politics seem to demand that we share the same viewpoint and the same methods, nature teaches us that diversity creates a healthy, balanced ecosystem. The courageous work that is done by those who get arrested for insisting on treaty rights is complemented by the equally courageous work of those who stay home to raise healthy children or who speak their poetry in front of an audience. Even the ones who remain silent and those who retreat into addiction have a place in this struggle by reminding us of the pain they carry from our shared history.

In that shared history, there is joy and beauty as well. Early one spring morning in 2011, hundreds of Native people dressed in their brightly colored regalia walked down Franklin Avenue to celebrate the kick-off of

Minnesota's American Indian month. Behind the honor guard, the eagle staffs, the jingle dresses, and the ribbon shirts came a small group of teenagers carrying a banner for the Dream of Wild Health farm.

Later that morning, our teens performed a skit they wrote about the importance of traditional foods and a healthy lifestyle. Overcoming their anxiety at performing in front of a large crowd, these young people spoke their truth to the community. Nearby, inside the Minneapolis American Indian Center, nearly forty organizations provided information on improving the health of Native people. Parents pushed strollers down crowded aisles, adults checked their blood sugar at the community clinic table, and everyone shared a feast.

There are other signs of change as well. The Osseo School District's "Success for the Future" program has graduated 100 percent of their nearly two hundred Native students for the past six years, compared to the state's overall graduation rate of 41 percent for Native students. Using an intergenerational cultural approach, Indian education for Osseo schools has shifted from teaching *about* Native culture to teaching *through* Native culture.

In Waziyatawin Angela Wilson's book, *What Does Justice Look Like?*, she defined a vision for justice in Minnesota that is rooted in her identity as well as in her scholarship as a Dakota historian. Having articulated that vision, she is equally committed to the work of educating all Minnesotans about the need to actively support justice for the Dakota Oyate and to putting herself on the front line. Her work pushes me to define my own vision for justice rather than floating along in a "colonial slumber."

As a grandmother, I have seen how small changes over time can slowly add up to big shifts in the broader community, just as incremental movement in tectonic plates can one day create an earthquake. Choosing to be healthy, rebalancing the physical dimension of the medicine wheel, is a fundamental first step toward Dependability. Returning to indigenous foods is an act of resistance against the commodity foods and inequitable food system that has ruined the health of so many Native people.

In my family, most of us have experienced some form of diabetes. Rather than allow this disease to become yet another label for Native people, justice means helping the Native community restore an indigenous relationship with plants that respects their importance in nurturing our bodies. Not from a place of shame and guilt but by relearning cultural teachings about health, including gratitude for the gifts we receive from the plant nation.

When my daughter joined the military in college, she stood up for values that seemed, on the surface, to challenge the way she had been raised—growing up in the arts community and attending antiwar rallies. Her decision shook my peace-loving aesthetic to the core. Yet as I supported her in making that choice, I saw how she retained her gentle nature as a peacekeeper while demonstrating her willingness to fight to defend herself, her family, and her country. In that balance, she exemplified the essence of a Dakota warrior. And that, I believe, is what we need to bring to the challenges we face: the loving heart of a peacekeeper and the fierce courage of the warrior or the Mother Tiger, as Gaby's family has demonstrated.

We will need to be at our best for the work that lies ahead; whether that means asserting our treaty rights, raising our grandchildren, preserving old seeds, or challenging institutional racism—the issues that surround us are immense. Native people continue to be under siege for their land, their resources, and their spirituality.

In 2009, the Internal Revenue Service auctioned off 7,100 acres of land belonging to the Crow Creek Reservation, citing failure to pay overdue employment taxes. Crow Creek is considered one of the poorest reservations in the country, with 70 percent of its members living below the poverty line. The Bureau of Indian Affairs had advised Crow Creek that it was exempt from federal employment taxes. The IRS seized land that was designated for a wind farm to provide jobs for people suffering from 80 percent unemployment. Fortunately, Crow Creek was later able to purchase the land back with a loan from the Shakopee Mdewakanton Sioux Community.

In Minnesota, Dakota people continue to battle to protect sacred sites, including Coldwater Spring, which the National Park Service refuses to acknowledge as sacred to the Dakota; Pilot Knob, *Oheyawahi*, renamed by Chris Leith and Arvol Looking Horse as Wotakuye Paha, the hill of all relatives, where a townhome development was narrowly defeated; and Fort Snelling. In an editorial letter written during Minnesota's sesquicentennial, Jeffrey Kolnick, associate professor of history at Southwest Minnesota State University, argued that Fort Snelling be moved from its site and rebuilt elsewhere, with a Minnesota Museum of Genocide constructed in its place. The area of Bdote, where the Mississippi and Minnesota Rivers come together, would become "a monument to the living memory of the genocide that gave birth to our state and to suffering of other peoples who have also been victims of genocide."

Yet these few examples don't begin to touch the breadth and depth of challenges that face Native people every day. Nor do they reveal the extent to which Native people are fighting back, taking charge of their well-being by creating programs to protect the language, educating families on historical trauma, teaching parenting skills, sharing lessons on handwork, drumming, and making regalia. A new land-based school for Dakota students in Minneapolis, Bdote Charter School, is in the planning stages. Even the obstinance of students who refuse to bend to school authority suggests a core of resilience that will not be broken. As do the young mothers who set aside time for retreat, seeking the silence they know will restore their spirits and help them raise healthy children.

Native people are also beginning to share their hard stories and confront abusive situations. The Boarding School Healing Project is documenting stories from former students who find it easier to face the past when they understand that what happened at many of these schools was a violation of human rights. By framing their experience from this perspective, people feel less shamed and find it easier to talk about these issues. Sharing these stories provides an opportunity for communities to begin healing as well as develop a national coalition of tribes and organizations who are working for reparations.

Unlike Canada and Australia, who share the United States' history of establishing a brutal residential school system, this country has yet to address this issue. In 2006, the government of Canada made a formal apology and passed legislation providing reparative payments and programs.

In 2008, the prime minister of Australia apologized to aboriginal communities, specifically for the abuses committed at residential schools. Yet the United States continues to ignore the consequences of this history while sanctioning other countries for their human rights violations. There are hopeful signs, however, that more Native people are willing to speak the truth and help us move forward.

In 2011, a landmark settlement was announced that called for the Society of Jesus in Portland, Oregon, to acknowledge their sexual abuse of Native students at the St. Mary's Mission and School near Omak, Washington. The Jesuit-run boarding school must pay $166 million to roughly 450 Native complainants, all from tribes across the Northwest. It took just one woman who refused to be a victim any longer to stand up and lead the way for hundreds more to fight back. While a monetary award is incidental to healing, the act of sharing these stories and insisting on justice is a first step toward restoring spiritual and emotional health.

And that, perhaps, is the most important step of all: defining justice in a way that is rooted in your own life and working to defend it. For each of the people interviewed in this book, there came a time when they too had to decide to stand up for themselves, for their cultural identity, and for their communities. They had to discover their gifts and the purpose they were given to do while resisting the negative messages that bombard Native people from every direction.

From Harley and Sue Eagle, I've learned the importance of applying critical analysis to the issues that surround us while developing authentic relationship skills and process. They have created a family system that incorporates their work as they continue to support indigenous people and issues in both the United States and Canada.

Clifford Canku is a first language speaker whose ability to see through to the essence of issues allows him to walk in both worlds as a spiritual leader and a minister. As a teacher, he helps students find a place to begin recovering their cultural identity. His work in translating the Dakota prisoner letters is a priceless gift to the Dakota community.

An artist and poet, Gabrielle Tateyuskanskan expresses her love of the land through her artwork and her activism while maintaining her family at the center of all that she does. Her leadership comes from a deep commitment to her own spirituality and her understanding of trauma and forgiveness. She is a tireless, compassionate educator.

Delores Brunelle's lifelong experience working with traumatized Native children helps her raise her grandson to be a healthy, happy human being. She is an artist with a gift for poetic language and a profound ability to create relationships with the natural world.

And Alameda Rocha's walk in this world demonstrates the power of faith to help us heal from even the most traumatic loss. Her generosity in sharing her knowledge with others who are struggling and her strong intuitive understanding of people demonstrate the innate kindness and hospitality of the Dakota.

I am indebted to all of them for the gifts they have shared.

My hope is that one day all of these efforts will be enough to create an earthquake, so that as a state, and as a country, we acknowledge the harm that has been done to Native people and especially to the children. In the words of the Lakota Chief Sitting Bull, "Let us put our minds together and see what life we can make for our children."

Imagine what that life would look like for our children if we were all doing our best to live up to our spiritual traditions. Not in the way of allowing manmade prayers to substitute for God's voice, but in truly entering into the Silence where we cry to God in prayer. A world where our compassion was so complete that we worked together to protect the earth and those less fortunate than us, and we forgave our enemies. A world in which all gods were tolerated, knowing that they are all part of an inexpressible, unknowable, Kind-Hearted Great Mystery.

A gust of wind would blow from one corner of this country to the other, sweeping away the misery and the grief and the horror. I imagine the relief of our ancestors in knowing that their suffering and their prayers inspired their descendents to return to the original recipe so that future generations would always be cared for. There will be peace, finally, when we all understand that we are born sacred and that each one of us is, and has always been, a Beloved Child.

ACKNOWLEDGMENTS

Wopida tanka eciciyapi ye!

This book belongs, first and foremost, to the people who believed in this work and shared their stories with me: Glenn Wasicuna; Harley, Sue, Danielle, and Emma Eagle; Clifford Canku; Gabrielle Tateyuskanskan (also Yvonne Wynde, Lisa Lopez); Delores and Dolton Brunelle; Alameda Rocha (and her relatives) and Naida Medicine Crow. My deepest thanks to all for opening their hearts and minds and allowing me to share their stories.

Special thanks to the people who helped me believe in this project, especially during the early days: my brother, Dave Wilson, who shares these journeys with me, reads everything, and speaks from his heart; and Carolyn Holbrook, my writing buddy. Nora Murphy and Denise Breton read several versions of the manuscript and asked the hard questions that pushed me to dig deeper.

My sister, Suzie, and my daughter, Jodi, provided encouragement throughout the years needed to finish the book. My patient husband, Jim Denomie, kept a path shoveled to my studio and inspired me with his art. Thanks to all of my family for their ongoing support, especially to Chuck, Cille, and Pauline, who are riders now in my spirit car.

I am indebted to everyone at Dream of Wild Health for the inspiration they provide and the good work that happens at the farm. Donna LaChapelle has been part of this book from the beginning—pidamaya ye for your loving kindness. I am grateful to all the people who have participated on the 2002–10 Marches and shared their stories with me.

Gwen Westerman's star quilt on the cover is the perfect artwork for this book. Thanks also to Joe Allen for creating thoughtful portraits for each person.

Many, many thanks to Ann Regan for giving me a deadline, asking good questions, and navigating sensitive issues with patience and integrity. I appreciate the efforts from all of the staff at Borealis Books who helped push this book through on a short timeline.

This book has also been supported with a Travel and Study Grant from the Jerome Foundation and writing residencies at Hedgebrook and Ragdale.

SOURCE NOTES

Where to Begin

Typically a speaker would introduce herself by telling where she is from, with specific reference to a reservation. My mother, Lucille Dion, was enrolled at the Rosebud Reservation, but my siblings and I are not. We are recognized as descendants of the Mdewakanton band. We are related to the LaCroix family who lived at Lower Sioux, Sisseton, and Santee during and after the 1862 Dakota War as well as the Frenier and Felix families. For a complete genealogy, please refer to my book *Spirit Car: Journey to a Dakota Past* (St. Paul, MN: Borealis Books, 2006).

Kids Today

Youth and health statistics summarized in Margaret C. Noreuil, RN, PhD, "Coming Full Circle: Understanding American Indian Health Disparities" (Nursing Education and Technology [NEAT]). Statistics on life expectancy, type 2 diabetes, and alcoholism from Indian Health Service, http://www.ihs.gov/index.asp. Information on youth poverty from U.S. 2000 Census. Dropout rates from October 30, 2006, press release issued by American Indian Higher Education Consortium (AIHEC). See also National Center for Education Statistics, http://www.nces.ed.gov.

To learn more about Native teen suicides, see "Native Tribes 'Losing Kids Every Day' to Suicide," by Dan Gunderson (Minnesota Public Radio, June 15, 2005), http://news.minnesota.publicradio.org/features/2005/06/10

_gundersond_indiansuicide/ : "Across the nation, American Indian teens commit suicide at a rate at least twice the national average. The rate is much higher in the Upper Midwest and Great Plains, where it's five to seven times higher than the national average, according to an official with the federal Substance Abuse and Mental Health Services Administration."

For information about terminator seed technology, see International Seed Federation, "Position Paper of the International Seed Federation on Genetic Use Restriction Technologies," adopted at Bangalore, India (June 2003), http://www.worldseed.org/isf/on_sustainable_agriculture.html. Monsanto grower agreement, http://www.monsanto.com/food-inc/Pages/seed-saving-and-legal-activities.aspx.

Chief Luther Standing Bear, *Land of the Spotted Eagle* (Lincoln: University of Nebraska Press, 1933), 330.

Eugene Anderson, *Ecologies of the Heart: Emotions, Belief, and the Environment* (New York: Oxford University Press, 1996), quoted in Gary Nabhan, *Enduring Seeds: Native American Agriculture and Wild Plant Conservation* (Tucson: University of Arizona Press, 1989), 84.

Andrea Smith, "Soul Wound: The Legacy of Native American Schools," *Amnesty Magazine,* available: http://www.racismagainstindians.org/AcademicPapers/SoulWound.htm.

In Harm's Way

John Fire Lame Deer with Richard Erdoes, *Lame Deer, Seeker of Visions* (New York: Simon & Schuster, 2001), 130.

Fort Ridgely stone circle: David Mather, "Deeper into History," *Minnesota Conservation Volunteer* (2010), http://www.dnr.state.mn.us/volunteer/julaug10/ridgely.html.

Three-fifths of world crops and potato information: Jack Weatherford, *Indian Givers: How the Indians of the Americas Transformed the World* (New York: Ballantine Books, 1988), 71.

"Vanishing Vegetables," *Foodlinks America,* The Emergency Food Assistance Program (TEFAP) Alliance Blog, October 8, 2010, http://tefapalliance.org/blog/archives/675.

Sacred science: Melissa K. Nelson, ed., *Original Instructions: Indigenous Teachings for a Sustainable Future* (Rochester, VT: Bear & Company, 2008), 12.

Deaths of 90 percent of Natives from disease: Guenter Lewy, "Were American Indians the Victims of Genocide?" George Mason University History News Network (January 22, 2007), http://hnn.us/articles/7302.html.

Quotation and healing process description: Maria Yellow Horse Brave Heart, "From Intergenerational Trauma to Intergenerational Healing," keynote, Fifth Annual White Bison Wellbriety Conference, Denver, Colorado, April 22, 2005, available: *Wellbriety! Online Magazine,* 6.6, http://www.whitebison.org/magazine/2005/volume6/no6.htm. For more information about Dr. Brave Heart, see http://www.columbia.edu/cu/ssw/faculty/profiles/braveheart.html. Other researchers doing compelling work on historical trauma include Dolores Subia BigFoot, PhD, Director, University of Oklahoma Health Sciences Center, and Karina Walters, PhD, University of Washington, Department of Social Work.

Conversation with student: adapted from my essay "Beloved Child," *Yellow Medicine Review: A Journal of Indigenous Literature, Art, and Thought,* Southwest Minnesota State University (Winter 2007): 170. My great-great-grandmother's encounter is related in Helen Mar Tarble, *The Story of My Capture and Escape during the Minnesota Indian Massacre of 1862* (St. Paul: Abbott Printing Company, 1904), 16–17.

Information about the 1862 Dakota War and the Dakota Commemorative March: Kenneth Carley, *The Dakota War of 1862: Minnesota's Other Civil War* (St. Paul: Minnesota Historical Society Press, 1976); Gary Clayton Anderson and Alan R. Woolworth, eds., *Through Dakota Eyes: Narrative Accounts of the Minnesota Indian War of 1862* (St. Paul: Minnesota Historical Society Press, 1988); Roy W. Meyer, *History of the Santee Sioux: United States Indian Policy on Trial,* rev. ed. (Lincoln: University of Nebraska Press, 1993).

Information on original prisoner number and deaths en route to Crow Creek and in first six weeks: testimony of John P. Williamson, "Condition of the Indian Tribes," Report of the Joint Special Committee (Washington, DC: Government Printing Office, 1867).

Williamson quotation and extensive information on Crow Creek and the Santee reservation: Meyer, *Santee Sioux*, 151.

Reference to children who died at Crow Creek: G. W. Knox, former superintendent of schools for the Winnebago Indians, to Bishop Whipple, March 25, 1864, Henry B. Whipple Papers, 1833–1934, Minnesota Historical Society, St. Paul.

David Wallace Adams, *Education for Extinction: American Indians and the Boarding School Experience, 1875–1928* (Lawrence: University Press of Kansas, 1995), 337.

Carl Schurz, "Present Aspects of the Indian Problem," *North American Review* 133.296 (July 1881): 1–24, http://www.trip.net/~bobwb/schurz /article/indian.html.

Richard H. Pratt, "The Advantages of Mingling Indians with Whites," *Americanizing the American Indians: Writings by the "Friends of the Indian" 1880–1900* (Cambridge, MA: Harvard University Press, 1973), 260–71, http://historymatters.gmu.edu/d/4929/.

Boarding school statistics, background, reports of widespread sexual abuse: "Soul Wound: The Legacy of Native American Schools," *Amnesty International Magazine,* available: http://www.racismagainstindians.org/Acade micPapers/Soulwound.htm.

Cemetery at Haskell Indian School: Boarding School Healing Project, http://www.boardingschoolhealingproject.org/.

Sexual assault rate study: U.S. Department of Justice, Office on Violence Against Women, "The Facts About Violence Against Women in Indian Country," http://www.ovw.usdoj.gov/ovw-fs.htm#fs-indian-country.

Tim Giago, "The Dark Legacy of the Indian Boarding Schools," *Huffington Post,* April 1, 2007, p.24. Giago was the founder and former editor and publisher of the *Lakota Times* and *Indian Country Today* newspapers and the founder and first president of the Native American Journalists Association. He was a Nieman Fellow at Harvard in the class of 1990–91. Clear Light Books of Santa Fe, New Mexico, published his latest book, *Children Left Behind.*

Sammy Toineeta quoted in Andrea Smith, "Soul Wound." More information about the Boarding School Healing Project available at http://www .boardingschoolhealingproject.org/.

Rachel Bennett, "American Indian Children in Foster Care," National Resource Center for Foster Care and Permanency Planning (2003), citing an earlier report published by the National Indian Child Welfare Association.

William Byler, "Destruction of American Indian Families," Association on American Indian Affairs (1977), 1–3.

Information on Indian Child Welfare Act: National Indian Child Welfare Association, http://www.nicwa.org/Indian_Child_Welfare_Act/.

Sterilization of Indian women: "Shattered Hearts: The Commercial Sexual Exploitation of American Indian Women and Girls," Minnesota Indian Women's Resource Center, Minneapolis (2009).

Native women experience the highest rate of violence; assault statistics: Lisa Bhungalia, "Native American Women and Violence," *National NOW Times* (Spring 2001).

Andrea Smith, *Conquest: Sexual Violence and Native American Genocide* (Cambridge, MA: South End Press, 2005).

United Nations, "Convention on the Prevention and Punishment of the Crime of Genocide," http://www.hrweb.org/legal/genocide.html.

Timeline

Basic timeline information drawn from http://www.america.gov/st/people
place-english/2008/November/20061106163901bpuho.5341455.html.

Indian Education Act, http://www.uintahbasintah.org/papers/indian
educationact.pdf.

Tribal Law and Order Act, http://www.whitehouse.gov/blog/2010/
07/29/tribal-law-and-order-act-2010-a-step-forward-native-women.

Harley and Sue Eagle

Ella Cara Deloria, *Waterlily* (Lincoln: University of Nebraska Press, 1988).

Kinship quotation: Ella Deloria, *Speaking of Indians* (Lincoln: University
of Nebraska Press, 1944), 30.

Joseph M. Marshall, *The Lakota Way: Stories and Lessons for Living* (New
York: Penguin, 2002).

1951 Indian Act, "Sixties Scoop," Kimelman quotation: John Steckley and
Bryan Cummins, *Full Circle: Canada's First Nations* (Toronto: Prentice
Hall, 2001).

2001 Truth Commission report: http://racismagainstindians.org/Acade
micPapers/Soulwound.htm. See also http://www.hiddenfromhistory.org.

Excerpts from Stephen Harper apology: http://www.cbc.ca/news/canada/
story/2008/06/11/pm-statement.html.

"Residential School Cash Has Deadly Fallout," http://www.canada.com/
calgaryherald/news/story.html?id=7c2678f1-fc12-4eab-bfbf-9f80b1e
49905.

Education for Native children is a complicated topic, but fortunately many
talented and passionate educators are working to improve conditions
within the public schools. I have worked with the Phillips Indian Educators (PIE) in Minneapolis to interview local elders on their experience and
best practices in teaching Native children. Transcripts and summary essays
are available at http://www.pieducators.com/wisdom/conversations.

Clifford Canku

Quotation from prisoner letters: Dan Gunderson, "Man Translates Letters of Dakota Imprisoned in MN," Associated Press, minnesota.cbslocal.com, 2011.

American Board of Commissioners, Riggs conversions: Raymond J. DeMallie and Douglas R. Parks, eds., *Sioux Indian Religion: Tradition and Innovation* (Norman: University of Oklahoma Press, 1987), 10.

Indian Religious Crimes Code: Lee Irwin, "Freedom, Law, and Prophecy: A Brief History of Native American Religious Resistance," *American Indian Quarterly* 21.1 (1997): 35.

Christianity in Native communities: Jacob Neusner, ed., *World Religions in America: An Introduction* (Louisville, KY: Westminster John Knox Press, 2003), 18.

"The Urban Relocation Program": available: http://www.pbs.org/indian country/history/relocate.html.

Number of language speakers remaining: Alliance of Early Childhood Professionals/Wicoie Nandagikendan, http://earlychildpro.org/revitailization/.

Gabrielle Tateyuskanskan

Waziyatawin Angela Wilson, ed., *In the Footsteps of Our Ancestors: The Dakota Commemorative Marches of the 21st Century* (St. Paul, MN: Living Justice Press, 2006).

David Martínez, *Dakota Philosopher: Charles Eastman and American Indian Thought* (St. Paul: Minnesota Historical Society Press, 2009), 6.

Severt Young Bear and R. D. Theisz, *Standing in the Light: A Lakota Way of Seeing* (Lincoln: University of Nebraska Press, 1994), 121.

Denise Breton and Stephen Lehman, *The Mystic Heart of Justice: Restoring Wholeness in a Broken World* (West Chester, PA: Chrysalis Books, 2001), 37.

Dakota males graduation rate: "South Dakota High Schools," Alliance for Excellent Education state cards, October 2010, http://www.all4ed.org/files/SouthDakota.pdf.

"Dakota 38 Documentary Remembers the 38 Dakota Executed in 1862," *The Circle,* February 11, 2011.

Delores Brunelle

Am Goyer, "Intergenerational Relationships: Grandparents Raising Grandchildren," *AARP International,* February 2006.

Dr. Vasant Lad, *The Yoga of Herbs: An Ayurvedic Guide to Herbal Medicine* (Twin Lakes, WI: Lotus Press, 1986).

Delores quotation (p. 133): from material written and synthesized by Delores Brunelle, M.A., A.T.R.; sources for this article include the NANA-COA training manuals written primarily by Jane Middleton-Moz, Annette Siquemton-Anque, and Anna Lattimer-Hanson.

Passive witnessing awareness: a concept articulated by Eckhart Tolle, *The Power of Now: A Guide to Spiritual Enlightenment* (Novato, CA: New World Library, 1999).

Alameda Rocha

Information on Chief Medicine Bear, Shields quotation: David Miller, Dennis Smith, Joseph R. McGeshick, James Shanley, and Caleb Shields, *The History of the Assiniboine and Sioux Tribes of the Fort Peck Indian Reservation, Montana, 1800–2000* (Helena: Montana Historical Society Press, 2008).

Deloria, *Speaking of Indians,* 28–29.

Marshall, *The Lakota Way,* 7.

A Silent Voice

Ohiyesa quotation: Charles Eastman, *The Soul of an Indian* (1911), quoted in Kent Nerburn, ed., *The Wisdom of the Native Americans* (Novato, CA: New World Library, 1999), 87.

Quotation on religion: Rosebud Sioux Tribe, http://www.rosebudsioux tribe-nsn.gov.

Phil Lane, Jr., Judie Bopp, Michael Bopp, Lee Brown, and elders, *The Sacred Tree: Reflections on Native American Spirituality* (Twin Lakes, WI: Lotus Press, 1984).

Osseo School District information: Priscilla Buffalohead and Ramona Kitto Stately, "Indian Education: A Culture-Based, Intergenerational Approach," *American Indian Graduate Center Magazine* (Fall 2010): 39, http://www .aigc.com/test.aigcs.org/04magazine/past/Fall10.pdf.

Colonial slumber reference: from "A Dakota Call to Consciousness," http:// waziyatawin.blogspot.com.

Crow Creek tax situation: blog post, Jason Wakiyan Thunderbird Spears, First Nations United, "Crow Creek and Coldwater Spring," March 22, 2010, http://minnesotahistory.net/?p=2380#more-2380.

Jeffrey Kolnick, "Fort Snelling on the Agenda," (Minneapolis) *Star Tribune,* February 17, 2008, http://www.startribune.com/opinion/15679667 .html?source=error.

St. Mary's Mission and School: William Yardley, "Catholic Order Reaches $166 Million Settlement with Sexual Abuse Victims," *New York Times,* March 25, 2011, http://www.nytimes.com/2011/03/26/us/26jesuits.html.

Beloved Child is set in the Arno Pro typeface family.

Book design and typesetting by
BNTypographics West Ltd., Victoria, B.C. Canada.

Printed by Thomson-Shore, Dexter, Michigan.